WILD
WANDERINGS
OF A
WORLDLY MIND

JAMES LEACH

WILD WANDERINGS OF A WORLDLY MIND

Self-published through Create Space

Self-published through Create Space
First Version

ISBN 9781517686642

Acknowledgements:

Thank you to my wife Cindy, of 51 years, for her spontaneous enthusiasm throughout my life! Don't miss "A Girl I Know" on page 132.

To Olga for her incredible sketches and persistance in her commitment to the project. Beautiful Olga dressed herself as a robot on page 51.

To Gianna Williams for her patience and diligence in assembling the book for production.

To Janet Bressler Ulane for her creative help with the book's title.

To Connie Harris for her valuable suggestions.

And to Cory Eggert for his encouragement and support in this entire endeavor.

Table of Contents

Humorous Witticisms

Winky and Looky Lola 12

Four Girls and a Truck!.. 14

Tormented Suitcase Lost His Wheel 16

Dance T-A-N-G-O 18

Santa's White Beard 20

The Bachelorettes.. 22

The Confused Duck 24

I Am a Bottle of Ketchup.. 26

Cute Girl in a Ferrari... 28

Always & Never 33

The Old Tramp.. 34

Corvette Drag Race 36

The Rejected Dog 38

Johnny and Me... 40

From the Desk of James Leach 45

The Dog, The Parakeet and The Stripper! 46

The Two Girls at the Bar 48

I Bought a Robot.. 50

A Coon Named Rac! 52

Join Me For a Riddle 54

Hyperboles From Italy & Beyond................................ 56

Do You Wash Between Your Toes?.............................. 60

The Casino Trip 62

"Rappin" With Jim & Cindy... 64

Table of Contents

Writings of Serious Prose and Poetry

The Rain is Coming! 68

Don't Cross This Cowboy............................... 70

A Brief Thought - Friendship......................... 73

911 World Trade Center 74

Questions From the Universe 76

Bullied 78

Machu Picchu and the Spaniards 80

A Water Buffalo Attacked Me 82

Church Camp... 84

The Sun Talks to the Earth 85

The Farmer & His Daughter 86

Stock Market Savvy 88

Check Out Girl 90

Antarctica Bound 92

100 Cities Around the World.......................... 96

It's a Conundrum to Me................................. 102

Ambulance Emergency................................... 104

Jim's Bus Driver Safety Speech....................... 106

The Old Indian Senses Danger 108

Our Journey Soon Ends................................. 111

It's a Motor Coach 112

The Night is Twisted....................................... 114

Walk to the Edge.. 116

Homesick Cruise Ship Girl 118

A Tribute to My Friends

My Friend - Stunt Pilot!................................. 122

A Girl I Know... 132

The Professional Lady 135

Randy Ketzner the Builder.............................. 136

Denelle Cuts My Hair 138

The Wedding in Scotland 140

RW Van Dyke - My Mentor 142

Chuck Shull Airline Pilot M-14...................... 144

Twenty Four
Humorous Witticisms

Winky and Looky Lola

Wacky Winky Watch Me, he lives in Blockerville.
It's a town near Void City, where you might seek a thrill.

Other places also close and fun to say the least,
Are Candyburg and Hungrytown where they often have a feast!

The area is quite secluded, so please don't let this out,
But Looky Lola Listen To Her is here without a doubt.

And Wacky Winky Watch Me, a showoff to be sure,
Thinks this Looky Lola Lady might be his only cure.

She has the knack and this I know, to talk consistently,
And gather a group of curious ones who want to hear and see!

Another man, whose name I'm told, is Seedy Silent Sam Shady,
He also seeks the amorous part of this lovely Looky Lady.

"The zebras have Dalmation dots and colored stripes as well."

And Seedy Sam lives now listen, in the darkest part of here,
It's in Scaryplace, with shades of red and orange and black I fear.

"Don't go to Scaryplace," I say, "It's not for young or old to find,"
A mystery surrounds this frightening land, and many there are not so kind.

Enough of bad, with so much good to fill our happy heads,
Let's check on Lola Listen To Her to see the man she weds.

But a meal we must encounter first, together we'll have a feast.
The rich the poor we all will dine, the hog is done now eat the beast!

The children play, Tommyboy and Sissygirl and Nancy all are there.
It's in the city of Fun We Have, it's a place where we all do care!

The animals thrive in this beautiful parish, here we show and tell,
The zebras have Dalmatian dots and colored stripes as well.

Horses here are mostly short, and friendly they seem to be,
They're close to the ground and when you stand, they don't even come to your knee.

Foliage and flowers are prevalent with many types of plants,
There are water bugs and dragonflies and sometimes biting ants.

The colors in this, valley are green with traces of mauve and yellow,
Reds and violets and pinks and beiges, but first did Lola, catch her fellow?

Looky Lola and the showoff Winky are in love, we do know this.
With Seedy Sam, who's dirty and mean, the lady would never have bliss.

Wacky winks at Lola, and pulls off his finger for she,
This trick wins Lola's heart for him, her answer forever will be.

"I love you Winky, I'll marry you," says Looky Lola, now Listen To Her.
And Winky smiles and listens to her, and smiles again still listening to her!

Four Girls and a Truck!

It's a pickup truck, it's owned by him, the hubcaps are shiny chrome.
The purchase is new, although it's used, the seats are leather and foam.

So fun this is, the title is his, can't wait to show it to Sharon!
Payments are high, he will work so hard, can't wait to show it to Karen!

Blacken the tires, the color is red, can't wait to show it to Teryn!
Stick on the floor, clutch it has, he definitely will show it to Erin!

This truck is hot, the tires will squeal, it's the closest thing to heaven,
On leather he rides in his pickup truck, we know this kid named Kevin.

A secret we have, but we must confess, the engine is a V8 Chevy!
Not stock the motor, the river flows by, he is driving on the levy.

Roll windows down, let some air in this truck, the radio up and loud,
It's country rock and roll, let's dance, the music is from the cloud!

He did show his truck to Sharon, she said she did not like,
Karen dumped him also, said she'd rather be on a bike.

Teryn for sure would not get in his beautiful pickup
     truck,
Last shot was Erin if she didn't like, this time he was
     definitely stuck.

This supercharged truck could go quite fast, five
     hundred horse,
Down the track he raced so fun to drive, his foot
     controlled the force.

He called Erin, she turned him down, I guess this ends
     the day,
He's thinking now he will change jobs, could really
     use more pay.

The music plays in his truck, so great to hear Bob
     Marley,
His thoughts now, girls will like, this truck he'll trade
     for a Harley!

Tormented Suitcase Lost His Wheel

A suitcase I am, but I've lost a wheel,
I'm crippled and limping, how clumsy I feel!

Rolling with grace to the airport I came,
Now dragging one corner and covered in shame.

They hit me; they threw me and slammed me with force!
My dignity compromised, they had no remorse!

Starting my vacation, three weeks are ahead,
Other luggage so attractive, I wish I was dead!

I saw her today, four casters she had,
How graceful she rolled, my thoughts are so bad!

Her beauty is blue, drab green I display,
Red ribbons her mark, impress her oh nay!

High dollar she is, in the taxi she goes,
Her route is a puzzle, not one of us knows.

From baggage claim, I am taken,
Scratching the floor I am visibly shaken.

Embarrassed oh my, get me to a car,
I'll hide in the trunk, our journey's not far.

In hotel storage, how could it ever be?
Her body is pressed tightly against me.

On her back I would like to flip her.
Forget my wheel, she's looking at my zipper!

Dance T-A-N-G-O

May you dance the Salsa, Oh Yes,
Do you prefer the Tango, I guess!
Foxtrot I love, the Cha Cha my dear,
Shall we dance dear girl, just look in the mirror.

Your form my lady is way at the top,
Whether you Rumba, Cha Cha or do the Bop!
This hobby of ours, dancing we love,
It's a gift from heaven, a gift from above.

Lindy, West and East Coast Swing,
Gather round me people, let me hear you sing.
Let yourself go, the Charleston my dear,
This dance, fantastic, let my partner draw near.

Do you also tap, not a surprise at all,
Clickety Clack you are a doll!
Your tap shoes girl, did you buy in town?
They're lovely I say, also your gown!

It's swing man, gangster attire,
Bring suspenders or what you desire.
Rat a tat tat, machine guns you know,
Forget the dance, let's face the foe!

This is nonsense man, get to the point,
These gangsters now are all in the joint!
Go back you to the dance hall indeed,
Let's buy this place, we now own the deed,

To the largest saloon and dance hall in town.
Shuffle Ball Change, put your foot down.
A Tequila Sir, prepare for Spain,
The Tango my lady, it is not in vain!

Sweep across the floor, let's go,
T...A....N...G....O!
Ball Room, Foxtrot, Big Band for me,
It's competition now, just pay your fee!

You win you lose, who cares we do!
Give it your best, you would we knew!
Dancing Oh My, How did this begin?
I don't know for sure, we did want to win.

It was fun, the competition I say,
We gave it a hell of a run today.
Our friends they performed, we all did our best,
This weekend I say, was quite a fest!

The dance floors are waiting throughout the land,
The cruise ships my lady, just give me your hand.
May you dance off the planet to the ends of the earth,
These dances we love, I believe from our birth!

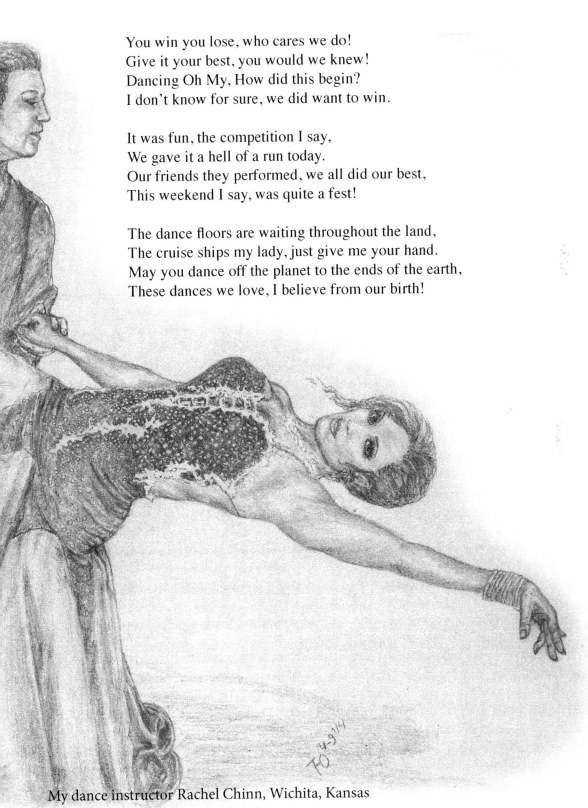

My dance instructor Rachel Chinn, Wichita, Kansas

Santa's White Beard

If a poem I could write that would be endeared;
Was about none other than Santa's white beard.

Some people say it's made out of snow.
The color is right, just wouldn't you know.

I think the color is because of his age.
Am I thinking right, are we on the same page?

Others would have you believe for sure,
His whiskers are soft like a polar bear's fur.

This I believe and I do here confess,
As a child I felt it, and soft I say yes!

There's much discussion about the beards length.
Is it measured in inches, wisdom or strength?

Rumors are about and it might be the case,
A billon names connect the beard to the face.

If my word, the beard would be shaved,
All the kids' names would not be saved.

The names for all the gifts would be lost,
A terrible disaster, oh what a cost!

But listen to me, I'll tell you right now,
His beard is protected, but I do not know how.

There are some things we don't understand.
Cause Santa's forever, that's why he's so grand!

The Bachelorettes

My name is Jim, I'm your driver tonight.
You're all so cute, it's quite a delight!

There's a party in town that just won't wait.
Let's get on the road so we won't be late.

Tonight I'm your slave, your standards will be met.
Your requests are important, this you can bet.

I'll drive you safely from bar to bar,
A bus is much safer than a car.

You rule the world, I'll take on all bets,
Because this we know, you are bachelorettes!

The Confused Duck

The duck is confused, we're sure of that!
We question his age and look at his hat.

The bill of his cap is turned to the back.
The desire to be young, he does not lack.

Elderly yes, he walks with a limp,
His body distorted, but he is not a wimp.

Though his feathers look old and some falling out,
His demeanor is youthful without a doubt!

At first, pity just comes to our mind.
But after observing, he's one of a kind!

This duck doesn't know he's getting old,
I can't figure out why he hasn't been told.

If he's not aware of the predicament he's in,
The experience of old age may never begin!

Hurry go tell him, point out his mistake.
The truth he must know, it's for his own sake!

I Am a Bottle of Ketchup

I am a bottle of ketchup, sitting, where I was placed,
The mustard stands beside me, this is where we're based!

I'm very well liked, all my friends are here,
Feel sorry for the mustard, not as good I fear!

She is the mustard and not sweet at all,
She is always present, but seldom gets a call!

Being the ketchup in this bottle of glass,
I am sometimes abused and hit on the ass!

Quit shaking me lady, patience my request,
I am known to splatter, you are nicely dressed!

Don't jam that steak knife down my throat please dear,
It's dangerous but the butter knife, I do not fear!

You are spanking my bottom, this is crazy I know,
So jealous the mustard, she keeps me in tow!

The salt and the pepper, they are also our friends,
They are shaken so much, confused it depends!

The napkins sit quietly in their chrome container,
Their skills are quite low, it is a no brainer!

Get ready, here comes the burger and fries,
The customers are grabby, and they tell many lies!

So my favorite color is red of course,
I'm splattered all over, everywhere I endorse!

Fingers I cover, lips and some cheeks,
I cover the counter, a rag the girl seeks!

What a day it has been, my cap has been lost,
My butt has been spanked, and my body's been tossed!

These people are crazy, show respect next time,
I know you love me, but abuse is a crime!

Cute Girl in a Ferrari

An unusual sight, a carrot with ears,
So sad to see, my eye fills with tears!
This carrot is tall three feet in height,
Let's shorten him up; I'll take a bite!

It's comedy just kidding, feel sorry for him,
A watermelon for one ear, his future is dim.
We judge in haste, the other ear a radish,
Hideous yet funny, for him we will wish,

A head that is normal, balanced each side,
But nature won't have it, the carrot must hide!
His top half is different now look at his legs,
Ugly roots go down, mercy he begs.

Birds eat the watermelon, seeds to the ground,
Sprouting with legs, new life they have found!
A parade springs up, the carrot in front.
The seeds are excited, activity they hunt!

Birds eat one ear, seeds running behind,
Insults we could make, but let us be kind.
It's a cucumber now look, it goes straight out.
Quite small a pickle, his nose don't doubt.

Smacked in the eye, black olive is one,
Green is the other, red pupil how fun!
A Ferrari pulls up, window rolls down,
Cute girl is the driver just came from town.

Believe this no way, romance in her mind?
The girl likes the carrot, this we do find!
The car door swings open, invitation is heard,
In comes the carrot, the seeds and a bird.

Stick shift on the floor, engine wound tight,
Girl kisses the carrot and takes a small bite!
The clutch pops out, white smoke from each tire,
So excited the carrot, his heart is on fire!
(continued)

Much enjoyment the seeds, as they sit on the dash,
Best view out the window, but first in a crash!
The carrot his day has improved so much,
Cute girl and her kisses, a magic touch.

Remember the radish both red and white,
Girl nibbles on this ear, what a delight!
The Autobahn is here, our speed will excel,
Terrified on the dash the seeds start to yell.

The bird flies around, the girl he upsets,
The window goes down and freedom he gets!
A siren is heard, the cops are coming,
Cute girl checks the mirror, the carrot is humming.

No speed limit here, what could be wrong?
Red lights are approaching it won't be long!
Police to cute girl, "You're driving too fast!"
"I'm sorry sir, was it you I passed?"

"Okay lady just checking it out,
Wild, rumors are floating about!
Why are the watermelon seeds in the car?
They look exhausted and not up to par."

"Officer we're friends and all doing fine.
The seeds are together, but the carrot is mine."
The discussion is over, the girl drives away,
The carrot so happy what a day!

Everyone relieved they won't go to jail.
Celebration is planned, our party won't fail.
A dance would be good with food and some drink.
The girl who is driving from the carrot gets a wink!

The band starts to play, grab a partner let's go.
The bird comes with a date wouldn't you know!
The carrot grabs the girl, new vigor he has found,
They twirl and they spin to the band what a sound!

Let me say fifty, seeds in all,
They're having a blast, they're having a ball!
The birds dance around, but now they search,
For the horn players head that's where they perch!

This dance I might say is out of hand,
They're drinking too much, please do understand!
Cute girl and the carrot, just close your eyes,
Some people are watching, I hear their sighs.

It was love at first sight, how lucky they are,
Other dates at this dance are not up to par!
Forget this talk, a party we share,
The birds, the seeds, we all do care.

In Germany they are, on the Autobahn they came,
The girl and the carrot, not sure what their game.
Let's see some of Europe from Munich they start,
Stuttgart and Frankfurt, to Cologne they will dart.

Amsterdam for now, this must be their goal,
They need a rest, these miles take their toll.
This group in the car, together they stay,
Friends they've become like a sunshine ray.

To this city they arrive, temptation is here,
Forget the drugs, please stick with beer,
Park this Ferrari, just take a walk,
District of Red Light, this place does rock!

Their tour must end in this interesting town,
Squeal the tires, put on your best gown!
South to Paris the glamour of it all,
Champs Elysees, he takes her to the ball!

The carrot observes the beauty of her hair,
Moulin Rouge they attend, love floats in the air,
Crazy Horse no way, nude dancing oh my,
The beauty, their forms, Jack and Coke, they're high!
(continued)

31

The seeds love Paris, the birds do for sure,
Fabulous this trek, like a kitten they purr.
Throttle to the floor, our tires they do smoke,
Black rubber, the pavement, twelve pistons do stroke.

Intake, compression, power, exhaust,
With Ferrari I say no power is lost.
Love, an affair, to London they head,
This lady and the carrot, they must be wed!

Piccadilly Circus, please park this car,
No marriage for a carrot, please find them a bar!
Scotch on the Rocks, what now is their plan?
Las Vegas the states, they'll see you're a man!

The seats on the plane, more tickets they buy,
Their friends they must take, they love to fly.
A chapel for weddings in Vegas they find,
This marriage I know is one of a kind!

Dedication, romance, this couple's in love,
They seem directed from a power above,
A kiss, a smooch, I do it is said,
Cute girl and the carrot just now they are wed!

All people are different the world around,
Unusual attraction this couple has found.
Sometimes we judge others in haste,
Like wine, each person has his own taste!

Always & Never

Always and never, these two words are trouble,
Usually and seldom, these won't break your bubble.

Always gives you no retreat, you're stuck with what you said,
Never leaves one no escape, you might go in the red!

If it happens nine times in ten, always will not work!
Accusations you receive, critics then will lurk!

Never, is a remark that's used, frequently made in haste,
Retreat from this you cannot do, with doom your tongue is laced!

The art of conversation, facets exponential.
Don't speak too soon I warn, you'll lose your keen potential!

Rhetorical competition does not control the day,
Relax just talk enjoy, no pressure you must pay!

To compete and argue, we say sometimes are fun,
But content and happiness, are best when day is done!

The Old Tramp

The old tramp sat on the curb thinking his life was fine.
He lived alone and was on the street since the age of nine.

No house he had, no rent he paid, this was one of his perks.
A cardboard box sometimes his home, often when winter lurks.

The tramp's best friend, the dog he had, a leash connecting them,
A grocery cart, this was his truck, blessings followed him.

A house he'd lived confined too much, freedom on the street,
People he watched, experience he had, this life could not be beat.

His favorite spot, the corner he sat, colored was his attire,
The dog was cute, people watched, money did they acquire!

Time for lunch, fun this was, a sandwich shared with the dog,
This afternoon they'll start again, a note was put in his log.

Under the bridge they go tonight, the dog and tramp meet friends,
With interest we observe it all, this poem I say now ends!

Corvette Drag Race

March is too early, the track is cold,
Who cares we'll race, let the story unfold!

Can you believe this traffic, just stay in line,
Will we get to race this car of mine?

It's not a sling shot, the car we race,
We're peons here, but give us some space!

An hour or two we will have to wait,
Big boys go through, then they open our gate!

No way, match me with the car right there?
A blower he has, this can't be fair!

I agree, his appearance is not that great,
It's obvious though, I have met my fate!

Beware of this maverick, super charged he is,
In Spain he raced, the town Cadiz.

His fenders are rusted, his car seems a wreck,
Money to his engine down the track this trek!

Okay I agree, to the line we approach,
Surrounded, young men they are my coach!

Yellow, yellow, yellow, green,
Reflex old man, you're not a teen.

The clutch pops out, the tires they spin,
The noise screams out, we want to win!

New sports car racing powerful junk,
His tail lights I see, I think we're sunk!

These men that race, dedicated they are,
Information I'll glean, we'll meet in the bar!

The Rejected Dog

He dumped me in the country, this my master did,
What did I do to him to make my presence rid?

I always loved my master, in his truck I liked to sit,
If I couldn't hang my head out, I always threw a fit!

Just one time I'm thinking back about a month ago,
I pooped upon the master's couch, I really just had to go!

That cat they have I can't believe, snooty she has to be,
I wish some Tom would get to her, this I'd like to see!

I always loved my master, things didn't have to change,
But the more I watched and noticed, something was very strange!

The number of people who came to the house, no you cannot guess,
Pap-a-raz-zi I am not, but they often did, cross dress!

A car is slowing the lady smiling, another chance is mine;
Lucky for me a Cadillac, in her kitchen tonight I'll dine!

Johnny and Me

One night while deep in slumber, or maybe it was before waking up in the early morning. I dreamed I was beginning life as a child, but my mind contained the wisdom I would possess as an old man.

The scenes of my life began to roll before me as if I were watching a video on a big screen television. The show started Thanksgiving Day when Johnny, my two-year-old toddler friend, leaned against that old kitchen stove, immediately after mom pulled the turkey out of the oven. He screamed like he had been popped on the bare bottom with a big flat board. I was amazed at the kid's stupidity; everyone knew how hot those old stoves get once you start cooking. It was only a week later and little John, as his dad called him, bounced off the bumper of one of those little Italian Fiats right after the wind blew that big yellow beach ball across the lawn and out into the middle of Third Street, with Johnny marching after it. My older sister Janey and I watched in awe from the safety of the curb, and we were bewildered by his spontaneous decision and lack of common sense.

Kindergarten was a breeze for me, but my good buddy continued to learn the hard way. His nose was constantly dripping, because he didn't wear a coat half the time. The mercury fell to sub-zero temperatures where we lived and blizzards were frequent. I usually watched the weather channel to help determine the proper clothing to wear.

I almost died laughing one day in third grade when Johnny decided to try smoking. He found this grungy old cigarette butt lying on the ground by the teeter totter. After brushing the dirt off and coaxing me to light it; he put on the most pathetic imitation of the Marlboro Man that you could imagine, ending with spasms of choking and coughing that would frighten any nonparticipant. Though I thought it to be one of the most hilarious times in my life I never smoked because I knew it caused cancer and emphysema and was a habit to avoid.

Johnny, by now my best friend, continued to be a source of humorous entertainment for me. He would get into more trouble than you could possibly contemplate, and I know it was only because he had no previous experiences like I had.

> *"You couldn't help but love the crazy jerk, but that boy had a lot to learn if he was going to live to be twenty-one."*

The day after school was out little John dove right off the spring board into the deep end of the pool. I assume he wanted to swim with the big kids. The lifeguard got him out of the water with one of those body hooks on the end of a long pole, and Johnny's dad called 911, or it probably would have been little John's last day on earth. I can still see him looking up at me after the paramedics revived him. Water sputtered from his mouth as that big contagious grin spread from one little fat cheek to the other. You couldn't help but love the crazy jerk, but that boy had a lot to learn if he was going to live to be twenty-one.

A few summers later, Johnny, Janey, and I went water skiing, and he laughed at the pink gooey sunscreen my sister and I put on.

He kept making fun of us and yelling, "Pinky, pinky!"

Janey and I got a beautiful tan, but before the day was over the little smart ass had two huge ugly water blisters that practically covered his whole back. The kid was so sunburned his mother told my mother that Johnny couldn't even put a sheet over himself at night because the pain was so excruciating. Those blisters broke the second day and Johnny got them terribly infected when he rolled around in the dirt wrestling that big old black lab they used to have; I am talking about the one with the grey whiskers and the long tongue dripping with saliva. Before that episode was over Johnny had to stay in bed two weeks that summer and he missed youth camp, and he missed canoeing, and he missed all those cute girls. My friend did meet the girls the next summer, and in fact, he married Jessica about ten years later. She was the pick of the whole camp.

Johnny loved to eat and he would saunter up to the burger bar with a direct order, "Give me a double quarter pounder and load it with the works!"

The works included: copious amounts of

> *"Both Johnny and I eventually took the form of fat little round roly-poly butter balls, and we didn't lose weight until later in life."*

ketchup and none of the other brand they call catsup, both sweet and dill pickles cemented in with an ample supply of juicy luscious relish, a thick slice of eye watering onion, a thick slice of bright red fresh non-hydroponic tomato, a thick layer of mustard oozing out the cracks and over the sides, and a layer of lettuce and sumptuous cheddar cheese placed between bun and burger on both sides. To coordinate the sandwich into a satisfying meal, Johnny would add a large order of curly fries, followed by a thick vanilla malt ingested with two flex straws and a long handled plastic spoon. I often laugh when I think of how I followed Johnny's example when it came to dining, even though I knew the consequences. Both Johnny and I eventually took the form of fat little round roly-poly butterballs, and we didn't lose weight until later in life when we were faced with high blood pressure.

The next anxious moment came when little hundred and eighty five pound John was a sophomore in high school, and he talked his dad into letting him buy that old Ford Thunderbird on time. The car was a faded red, and it had a vinyl top that was well weathered into a grey color, but with splotches of black still left like (continued)

"There was a long line of youth in front of Johnny's house..."

43

> *"I realized their minds contained the knowledge that would conquer many of the problems life had showered upon me."*

small islands across the roof. The edges of the vinyl had peeled up and started to fray, leaving an unkempt shaggy look around the back glass. The vehicle wasn't much, but it was Johnny's first car, and he did own it, and this proud owner was going to find out how fast his car could go around that curve between here and Eddyville.

Within the week Johnny rolled his Thunderbird three times trying to take that curve, just four miles this side of Eddyville, at a hundred and ten miles per hour! Neither he nor the boy riding with him were wearing seat belts. Both of them were injured seriously. Johnny had a compound femoral fracture and a nasty laceration on his forehead. Though he was on crutches for three months, Johnny told me later he was sure he would have made the curve at a hundred. I felt like Johnny was trying to pack a lifetime of experiences into his first fifteen years.

It was not long after he married Jessica that Johnny received an expensive education in the commodity market. He bought gold futures at the peak and just about lost his home and car before he got out of that mess.

I tried to tell him it was risky business, but he had to learn for himself. As time went on, Johnny became wiser at investing as well as everything else.

Waking up from my dream, I catapulted out of bed and rushed to my elders to listen, for I realized their minds contained the knowledge that would conquer many of the problems life had showered upon me. My elders were kind, and they talked with pride about the lessons they had learned, and they beamed with pleasure at the devoted attention I gave to their stories. Their knowledge had been gained the slow way, one experience at a time, building and adding to other experiences that continued to assemble a sagacious mind that could recall solutions to many problems.

One day I looked in the mirror, and was astonished to see time had passed. I stared at the wrinkled face and white hair, and I knew my time had come to be the speaker. There was a line of youth waiting to listen to me, because they, too, had come to realize the old people were very wise.

I looked out my window and across the street to where my best friend Johnny lived. There was a long line of youth in front of his house, for Johnny was considered one of the wisest men in the whole community. He always liked to show the young people the knife wound he got in California when he tried to tell those big dog Hell's Angels what they could do with their choppers!

FROM THE DESK OF JAMES LEACH

Reciprocate with conversation and learn to articulate by eloquent rhetoric, whether in vernacular prose or some other colloquial genre more indigenous to another time or culture.

The Dog, The Parakeet and The Stripper!

The dog and the parakeet, popcorn they did share,
Toy poodle was the dog, they did make quite a pair!

The stripper was their friend, and popcorn she could pop,
Among the friends she had, these two were at the top!

She'd take them to the club with her, the popcorn bowl she'd fill,
The bowl was placed upon the floor so the two would get a thrill.

The dog steps up, to the dish, to devour the buttered corn,
The bird flies down from his cage and treats the dog with scorn.

The fun begins, as the dog backs off, feelings hurt for sure,
The feisty bird, scolding he does, bombards the wretched cur!

The stripper yells to the other girls, come watch this funny show!
They gather round, all sparsely clad, laughing from head to toe!

The cautious dog, patiently waits as the bird stuffs itself,
Back to his house the bird flies, his cage sits on a shelf.

The dog returns to the bowl, to eat every last drop,
He'd like to kill the bird some day, but the stripper might call the cop!

This girl we know, who likes to strip, enjoys being on stage,
The attention she gets, so fun it is, more than just a wage.

Pole dancer she is, much practice she's had, the tips come rolling in,
Time to go home, the three of them, what a lovely day it's been!!

The Two Girls at the Bar

Two girls who work at the bar, their names I do not know,
No smile they give when they walk by, I feel so very low!

From Chile I know this one is from, Russia the other girl,
Thirty-three countries on this ship, the wine your toes will curl.

The one girl is quite tall, the other is tall as well,
Not sure how I can tell apart, please someone ring a bell.

Efficient yes, the energy of youth, we love to watch them go,
We like to guess what their lives are like, curiosity they do sow.

The world they travel, everywhere they go, at such an early age,
Bold they are, free spirits indeed, they have flown right out of their cage.

The girl from Chile, I talked to her, quite interesting is her life,
Brown hair she has, yes it is dark, and no not yet a wife.

The girl from Chile again is here, and volleyball yes she plays,
Fashion she loves, the dresses she wears, are bought in the Princess Cays.

Sophia from Chile

If beauty you want, make up she does, a man will love your look,
Zac Efron, her favorite star, please check your movie book.

Coca-Cola the bottle, we see it now, the shape this glass does take,
This lady, her figure, copies the design, genuine yes no fake.

The Russian girl, fascinating indeed, let's take a closer view,
The color she likes, pink is best, it's one of her favorite few.

Arabian Dancing this lady likes, she wears the classy shoes,
If you watch her dance, be careful now, you may just burn out a fuse.

Photography her hobby, men with muscle, just laugh out loud please.
A thong is worn, she loves the beach, either Cape Town or Belize.

A football fan, the teams she knows, at the game with tasty food,
Music is hers, all kinds she likes, just enjoy with her favorite dude.

The riddle is solved, so happy am I, their names do now come forth,
Anna from Russia and Sophia from Chile, friends from south and north.

Anna from Russia

49

I Bought a Robot

So fun this is, although it's pricey,
My new robot makes my life quite spicy!

Don't know for sure who invents these machines;
My floor is scrubbed and my house he cleans!

I call it a he, but the gender not known,
It seems quite formal, no way not a clone!

This creature is smart, and knowledge is the key,
I call her a she when the back rub's for me.

She drives my car never missing a turn,
I don't even drive, seems so hard to learn.

Everywhere they are, the robots I mean,
They visit, they talk, this much I have seen!

I've heard people say the world they will run,
It's hard to believe, they are all so fun.

They're quite sophisticated, they look like us,
You buy online, they're delivered on a bus.

They walk right off, on your door they knock.
They are just like humans the way they talk.

I own only one with a very low price,
I hope for better, it would be so nice.

Non violent robot, this one I like,
No bodyguard for me, just take a hike.

Many choices when you order, some standards not par.
Mine has good morals, so happy we are.

I was talking last week to my human friend,
Robots want to vote, a message they send.

Equal to us, a thought they can't detain,
Intelligent for sure, they passed the human brain.

Peaceful demonstrations they're having on the street,
Alarming rumors I have heard, here I can't repeat.

The weekends approaching, we continue, with life,
Upstate New York, we travel with no strife.

My job is secure, and I have no major loss,
Although I hear next Monday, a robot is my boss!!

A Coon Named Rac!

Abandoned he was, eyes were closed, only a few days old,
His mother now gone, he was left alone to slowly die in the cold.

Rescued he is by a lady that cares, this coon's name is Rac,
The fall he had, near death he was, the little guy fell on his back.

His leg was cut, the lady did see, and rushed him to the vet,
The vet to the lady, it is not wise to keep him for a pet.

The wound was stitched, the bill was high, no problem if you're kind,
She takes him home, eye dropper for food, the lady does not mind,

The little Raccoon, the milk he swallowed, and growth he soon displayed,
Mischievous pranks he cleverly did, his plans were always made.

His teeth were sharp, his movements fast, he usually washed his food,
She went to town in her pickup truck, sometimes Rac was rude.

Crowds would gather by her truck, to see little Rac, his charm,
Sometimes he bad and bite his guests, he meant to do them harm.

But disciplined he was, he never did pee in the pickup truck,
Drank his water, then straddled the dish, skill it was not luck.

Video she took of this clown with paws, he always wore a mask,
So fun he was, crazy oh my, keeping track of him a task.

People he loved, to the neighbors he'd go, first a hug then bite,
Her little boy became a man, personality left in the night.

She loved her guy oh so much, but things were out of hand,
To the country he must return, life's cycle ends with the land.

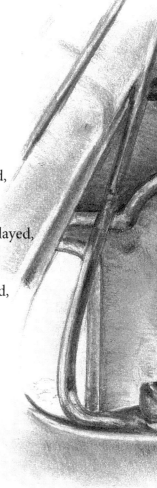

Join Me For a Riddle

I would like to become a riddle, join me for the fun,
Much salt, liked by me, blood pressure I have none.

The world's a playground, love to travel, must say I am driven,
Sometimes confused which way to turn, this fact's a given.

So strong I am, powerful indeed, please call me man of steel,
I could be hurt, trouble abound, come rescue soon with zeal.

Oh yes they say I am off, even at times they call me dizzy,
But I work so hard twenty four seven, and always stay so busy.

Have you figured me out or do you want more hints, this I can do,
Let me think what would work, I love so much the color blue.

A trick on you, thus I do hide, so cheating is not for you,
The riddle answer not on this page is cleverly hidden from view.

The answer you seek, important I am, a Princess so very stellar,
Hope you had fun with this riddle, I am the ship's ---------! (see page 147).

Hyperboles From Italy & Beyond

After navigating the streets of Rome by various conveyances, two quinquagenarians decided it would be challenging to rent a car and commingle with macho Italian drivers on their high speed Autostradas. Inexperienced American drivers often discuss these freeways with apprehension.

I questioned our taxi driver before renting a car, "What should we do if we have a collision; call the police?"

"No, No, No," he disgustedly replied.

I blurted out defensively, "We would in the United States!"

"For every crash?" he yelled with an incredulous expression. His words continued, "No, No, No, we have many wrecks, just exchange insurance papers and continue your journey!"

That night I had an unsettling knot between my esophagus and duodenum as I faded from insomnia to dreams of danger, trauma, and even death. Driving from alpha, the center of Rome to omega, anywhere outside the city appeared to be a monumental task equivalent to Lindbergh's crossing the Atlantic.

Disguised with a theatrical aura of confidence I would drive and Cindy, my wife, displaying unequivocal panic, would direct me through the maze to the Autostrada. We emerged from the underground parking to face what looked like a reincarnated World War II panzer division, but instead, was rush hour traffic in Rome! The Italians, as in other parts of Europe, enjoy a two hour break in the afternoon, creating four rush hours a day. The pandemonium crescendoed as we discovered the street names changed every other block; and even a prodigy could not study a map at that pace. After an hour of tenacious fortitude, we saw a sign clandestinely announcing "Autostrada," not "Racetrack-Heart Patients Prohibited." The infamous Autostrada turned out to be a wonderful highway including: slower cars and trucks behaving in the right lane, a 120 kilometer per hour unenforced speed limit, some autos traveling over 180 kilometers per hour (110 miles per hour), audaciously fast drivers flashing their lights to clear the way, and insane speed demons who continuously run their left blinker signifying they mean business and get the hell out of "their" left lane.

> *"I would drive and Cindy, my wife, displaying unequivocal panic, would direct me through the maze to the Autostrada. We emerged from the underground parking to face what looked like a reincarnated World War II panzer division, but instead, was rush hour traffic in Rome!"*

Following only one car length at 140 kilometers per hour (85 mph) is a natural phenomenon with Italian drivers. Because of this precarious intimacy between vehicles, often ending in an injurious affair, four way flashers, signaling in unison from here to infinity, (continued)

Venice

Florence

Pisa

ROME

Naples

Palermo

instantaneously acknowledge any break in the flow of traffic. When the problem diminishes, drivers simultaneously calm easily excitable blinking lights to a dull glow, anxious toes force accelerators to the floor, and the process of transportation begins again.

The next surge of adrenalin came when we stopped at a red light, as Americans are taught to do. To Italians, a stop light is only a suggestion and use them just for convenience, such as running in to pick up a bottle of wine. As we waited for the light to change, a loud noise reverberated from my left door, specifically near the area the rear view mirror previously occupied. The Italian driver who had sideswiped me, or possibly an American boldly impersonating an Italian driver, drove fearlessly on, hesitantly looking back as his BMW zigzagged slightly out of control, but well within tolerances allowed by men of steel. Cindy cautiously reappeared from below the dash, after competing with the carpet for space near the floorboards. She found me trembling as I manually rolled my window down (no radio or air conditioning either) to find the ingenious Italians had break away mirrors for such occasions and we and our unscathed vehicle could still travel. Reaching out and folding the mirror to its neutral position, I confidently proclaimed, with an expression often used in foreign lands where a large terminology in English is not popular, "No prob-a-lem!" We sped away from that intersection in Florence with true Italian vigor; feeling, if we so desired, we could probably conquer the world.

A ciphering aficionado's Mensa psyche will be challenged by trying to pay the Monte Carlo Autostrada toll in French francs, with a wallet containing Greek drachma, Italian lira, Austrian shillings, Swiss francs, and American dollars. Cognition is also im-

paired when aggressive honking suggests accelerating one's binary system into calculating foreign exchange rates. Humiliation comes quickly to an omniscient future currency trader, who asks for Australian shillings at an Austrian exchange window, (LOL) or who draws one tenth the cash he needs from an Athens ATM, because he believes 6000 drachmas appears adequate. Please check where the decimal point is located next time!

"We did not speed away from this scene with the confidence to conquer the world, but cautiously drove the first fifty kilometers below the speed limit, experiencing diaphoresis (shortness of breath), and an impending feeling of doom often associated with acute myocardial infarctions."

Between Christopher Columbus' birthplace and Rome we made a wrong turn and trying to avoid saying the word "lost" to my wife. I sheepishly admitted, "I cannot locate our position on the map." We soon forgot this conundrum, when several men emerged from two vehicles displaying the words "POLIZIA," and flagged us to the side of the road. An Uzi machine gun has a unique way of intimidating the most fearless of travelers, as it is held by a policeman standing in front of our radiator. A man's uncompromising eyes pierced the glass as I tepidly opened my window.

I yielded to his stern demand with the only Mel Tillis line I could think of, "You-you, wa-want my pa-pa-passport?"

After 300 seconds of a confused American-Italian vocabulary test, the uniformed carabinieri determined we were harmless American turistas driving back to our original destination, Rome. (No problem!) We did not speed away from this scene with the confidence to conquer the world, but cautiously drove the first fifty kilometers below the speed limit, experiencing diaphoresis (shortness of breath), and an impending feeling of doom often associated with acute myocardial infarctions.

"The challenge of conversing with the people, as one encounters dialects indigenous to different countries, is a delightful experience."

Most Europeans are bilingual; many speak four or five languages. The challenge of conversing with the people, as one encounters dialects indigenous to different countries, is a delightful experience. We found ourselves using only the subject and verb to get our point across, because any additional words confused the listener. After three weeks of practicing, we became so adept at this procedure, we subconsciously continued the process when alone. Instead of saying, "Please turn the television up," simply command, "TV-up!" also using a thumbs up signal! If the hotel concierge does not speak English say, "Bonjourno---dinner?" Use a newly acquired Italian word, meaning "good morning", use an English word one hopes they will recognize; use hand and eye signals demonstrating an eagerness to eat. This is not conversation, but it is stimulating communication. In most circumstances diners will soon be enjoying the hospitality of wonderfully courteous waitresses serving ambrosia as only the Romans can do.

After twenty three days and three thousand kilometers in a stick shift Fiat, a ragtag couple rolled into Rome, ignoring the armored vehicle and machine-gun turret guarding the entrance to Leonardo da Vinci Airport. Now seasoned veterans of this educational marathon, they had encountered anxiety and ecstasy from Mount Vesuvius to Innsbruck, from Athens to the Matterhorn and from Venice to Nice.

That reminds me; I was visiting with this sagacious old taxi driver in Athens and he told me that driving in Italy was effortless compared to driving in Turkey; and I was thinking about calling Jim & Cindy's Tours, and pricing two airline tickets to Istanbul!

Do You Wash Between Your Toes?

Do you wash between your toes I ask, curious this I am?
Did your Mother force this task on you, a curse me thank you ma'am!

A child at five a boy in dirt, separate two toes and look,
Oh my step back the subject filth, on this I could write a book!

Some mothers did not check the toes, these kids I say are blessed,
For years I washed between my toes, many times I have confessed!

Eight spaces there are between ten toes, this happens once a day!
Seventy years, three sixty five days, twenty thousand times let's say!

Twenty thousand, times eight spaces, one sixty thousand for sure!
One second per crack, two thousand minutes, please do listen sir!

Forty four hours in your life, just cleaning your toes,
At first I thought a waste of time, but listen now here goes!

I forgive you mom, this curse on me, I love my toes are clean,
Only four days in my life, others have missed, it does seem!

Many are us, this addiction we have, between our toes are slots,
Meticulous we are, laughing out loud, we do connect the dots!

If this curse you have, continue on, just clean your toes each day,
And if you do refuse this task, don't smell your toes, let's pray!!

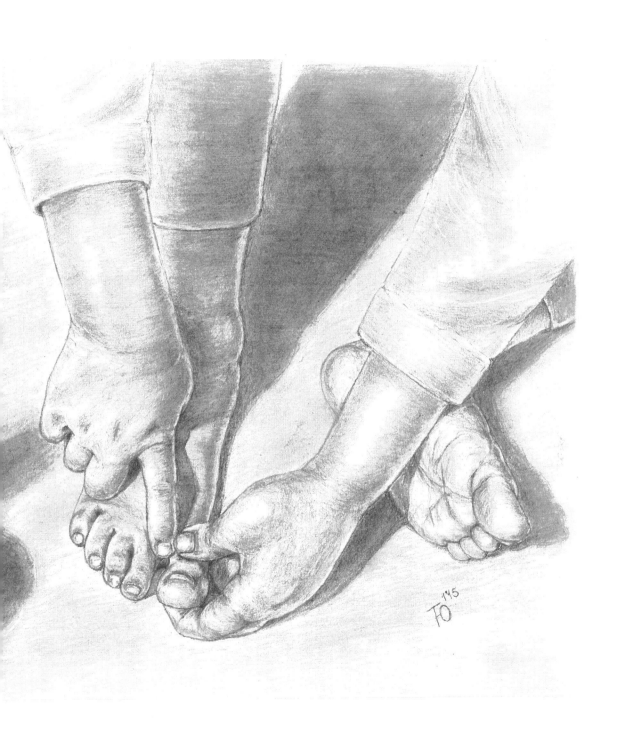

The Casino Trip

Jim is my name,
I'll tell you my aim.

To drive you today
Without losing my way.

Our journey begins
Fellow gamblers and friends.

The slots they await
As we bolt through the gate!

Our luck will be good,
As we know it should.

Our money will grow.
We'll come home with a glow.

I'm ready to play,
So get out of my way!

Our step-on-guides in many cities! From left to right: Bitsy, Chie, Cherry and Martha.

"Rappin" With Jim & Cindy

Jim and Cindy's Tours, that's what they say it is,
It's all on wheels and they make it real show biz!

Cindy entertains with all kinds of funny stuff,
From the auctioneer song to Henry in the rough!

Jim concentrates on driving this beautiful bus.
He wants you all comfortable so you won't raise a fuss.

Jim's favorite song is, "The Darktown Strutter's Ball."
Cindy sometimes sings it, oh isn't she a doll!

This I ask, haven't you been on a trip with us?
Just sit back, enjoy the day, you're riding on our bus!

"I'll be down to get you in a taxi, honey!"

Twenty Four
Writings of Serious Prose and Poetry

The Rain Is Coming!

The rain started not as drops, but a fine imagined mist,
A drop did fall, then two, the sidewalk so gently kissed.

Each drop spreads out darkening a spot with dryness in between,
These islands of water are joined by friends; their borders cannot be seen.

The city streets, dominated by grime, start to put on a smile,
Sprinkling at first, puddles are formed meandering down for a mile.

The rain continues, the drops are dancing, shaking hands throughout the day,
Opportunity knocks, umbrellas for sale, just how much will you pay?

People scurry, the scent of moisture, seems to please their mood,
In the country the farmers cheer, this rain will produce our food.

The rain bathes the city streets, and a small kitten does purr,
The sidewalks, a sea of umbrellas, the colors merge to a blur.

Car doors open and vehicles converge, cautiously to meet their fates,
The tempo increases and the heavens do, literally open the gates!

Emergency vehicles are rolling, as roads are beginning to flood,
Four inches of rain in three hours, the sewers are packed with mud!

Slowly moving this monster storm, and so gently it did begin,
A different route life sometimes takes, prepare to lose, but expect to win!

Don't Cross This Cowboy

He hit the doors, wide open they swung,
Whiskey he needed, his friend had been hung!
He'd get the bastards, time he could take,
They were heading south, plans he would make!

The drink swallowed quickly, he ordered another.
Kill them he swore on the grave of his mother.
The Scotch went down smoothly, bolder he became.
The gun in his holster he could readily aim!

Three drinks are now gone, she approached with ease,
Her eyes were unusual, her breasts were a tease.
"Hey cowboy, you're cute, what brings you to town?"
His reply, he was drunk, he gave her a frown!

Discouraged no way, she continued to pursue,
"Cowboy, upstairs, whatever you do?"
His face was leathered, deep scar so bold,
"Desire you my lady, no respect I withhold."

"But my friend is dead and revenge I do seek.
Kill them I will," not turning his cheek!
On his horse he rode, moving south.
The stallion was running, the bit in its mouth.

From Abilene they ran, Kansas I talk,
Their number was four, to the grave they would walk!
Several days in the saddle, Oklahoma passed by,
He followed at a distance, in Texas they would die!

Experience many years, this cowboy had had.
Shooting and fighting, he had started as a lad!
Kicked out by his Father at the early age of ten,
Prostitution his mother, who had laid many men!
(continued)

This boy now man, you can imagine was tough.
Don't cross him ever, are you ready for rough?
Forty four caliber, his revolver by Colt,
If you challenge this cowboy you start a revolt.

Confidence he had, he would choose the time.
Self defense it would be, this is not a crime!
Youth had gone by, aged he was now,
But reflex was quick to continue his vow!

Fort Worth he would choose, familiar this bar.
They sat at a table, he had traveled so far!
He stood and faced them and words they were said,
"My friend you have hung and now you are dead!"

Their pistols flew out, slow motion indeed,
Our cowboy like lightening, he drew a bead.
Their guns half drawn, he shot them all four,
Accusations he remembered, his mother was a whore!

His friend they had hung, let the truth be here,
The man was his brother, let's pray with a tear.
The old west was severe, much killing was done.
Geography carved out with a knife and a gun!

Our cowboy was one of many tough men,
Without them, where would this nation have been?
All races from countries near and afar,
We are different because everyone we are!

A Brief Thought - Friendship

A friendship originates in a flash of thought, an impulse
of brain waves, a minute whisper of intelligent imagination.
It's birth at zero, it builds from a grain of sand, composing
the pieces as the crescendo grows. Increasing, intensifying from
byte to megabytes, the power accumulates and concentrates
on the subject in a caring, loving manner, and is caused
by an unselfish attitude that is nourished by a look, a smile,
or a twinkling eye. It can happen in an instant and be cultivated
for a lifetime. It affects all ages and is immensely contagious,
spreading from person to person, continent to continent like falling
dominoes, in multicolors. Whether it comes in the name of
friendship, peace or love, it is spoken in a multitude of languages
and is a possession held by all classes of people. It is a powerful
source of energy, impossible to measure with scientific
instruments, and is tugging on the human race like the moon
pulls on planet earth. The future chapters since the birth of man
will be written on the faces surrounding us.

911 World Trade Center

Our country is America, the people, we are strong,

Push us to the edge, your decision will be wrong.

Resilience in our genes, we come from everywhere,

Adventure in our veins, a coat of tough we wear.

Gentle love we also have, a human kind of strength,

A better world that's safe, this we seek at length.

The many brave who gave their all, we honor from now on,

That sacrifice those heroes made, these people now are gone.

The tears will flow, this day is here, we say nine-eleven,

Three thousand dead and many more, they watch us all from heaven!

This poem was written on the 10th anniversary of Nine-Eleven.

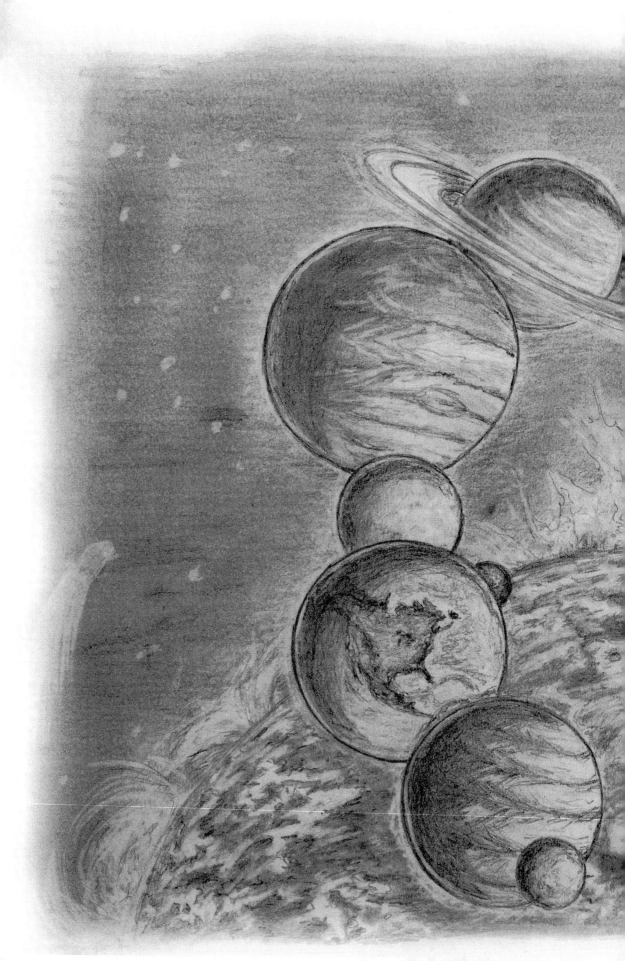

Questions From the Universe

Four and a half billion, the age of the earth,
Measured in years, we're starting from birth.
Fourteen billion, it's universe we're talking.
Check with the brilliant, maybe Stephen Hawking.

The Big Bang, if you believe, started back then,
Those facts or just theories, just where to begin?
A lecture I attended, now let me describe,
A fifty foot rope was stretched, do you jibe?

On a cruise ship so intriguing, just let me do tell,
Fourteen billion the rope I do yell.
Concentrate my friend, this story will proceed
Only two hundred thousand is man do you heed?

Six thousandths of an inch, on this fifty foot rope,
The thickness of a paper, human race, can we cope?
Men's time in existence against fourteen billion years,
We're a blip on the screen, let's pause and shed tears.

Science is there, many times we ignore,
It was shocking to me, my questions do soar!
We sometimes believe we're the center of it all,
But likely we aren't, I do say, King Saul!

Bullied

He was fourteen, had been bullied for years.
Suicide would be easy, he could hear the jeers!

Scars on his face and hair sticking out,
He'd been ridiculed forever without a doubt.

School had just started, his sophomore year.
He dreaded each day, he was filled with fear.

His confidence was shattered, cruelty to him.
How could he go on, his future so dim!

Someone please God, help this boy soon,
He's going for broke, he'll shoot the moon!

This person steps forward, a miraculous fact,
Approaches the boy, it's a courageous act.

"How are you today?" A conversation would be fun.
"What a beautiful day to bask in the sun."

"To school are you going, such a dreary place.
Let's escape you and me, I rest my case!"

An interest is sparked, our depressed boy responds.
"Thank you for asking." His emotion soon bonds.

It's fragile, a friendship, so wonderful indeed,
Let's continue this story, I will proceed.

A person was so kind to notice this lad,
Not for pity, but so genuinely clad!

From suicide to bonding these men are new friends.
Do you see in your surrounding how you can make amends?

I ask you my peer, it's kindness for our sake.
Love those who are bullied, a better world we make!

Machu Picchu and the Spaniards

Machu Picchu in Peru we know,
Built by the Incas, they had no foe.

A peaceful race, few weapons they had,
In the sixteenth century the results turn bad!

From Spain they came with a mighty force,
Guns and armor from a plentiful source!

Machu Picchu they did not find,
But to the Incas, the Spaniards weren't kind!

Let us go back to twelve hundred AD,
The Incas were brilliant, go visit and see.

Architectural accomplishments, unable to describe,
Remarkable feats were achieved by this tribe.

Huge stones with precision together were placed,
Tedious and accurate, nothing in haste.

The value of gold to the Incas was none,
For gold the Spaniards, everywhere would run!

Gold to the Incas ubiquitous oh yes,
From gold their horseshoes were made no less!

Can you imagine making horseshoes out of gold?
Remarkable stories start to unfold.

Living on a mountain, eight thousand feet high,
Oxygen not prevalent, I tell you no lie!

Their lungs were developed to accommodate this truth,
Also their hearts were larger from youth.

Today nearby, a city is there,
Eleven thousand feet, you gasp for air!

Cusco, Peru, we are talking about,
Inhale yes breathe, then stand up and shout!

The experience we had here, oh so fun,
From morning to night, we were on the run!

My friend go see, Peru just now,
Go in your youth, just make a vow!

No worry if your age is somewhat advanced,
The experience of breathing will just be enhanced!

A Water Buffalo Attacked Me

A safari we're on, Cape Town is near,
Our guide, no gun, I am filled with fear!
It's a truck we're in, the temperature is cold,
Only canvas on our side, no danger I am told!

Two elephants we see, a fight it is not,
How embarrassing the male, his demeanor is hot.
My pulse is racing, there are lions ahead,
Too close they are, no gun we're dead!

Our guide confesses last year a story,
A lion jumps the truck in all his glory!
Back tires on the truck are the goal,
Rubber is pierced, giant teeth take their toll!

Seven lions close to us, just ten feet away,
My heart is pounding, I'm going to pray!
Experienced the driver, truck parks on a hill,
The lions they watch and time stands still!

A water buffalo, in the road I see,
Most dangerous of animals, just let him be!
Our truck stops, only canvas on our side,
The bull starts charging, where can I hide?

Thirty people in the truck, the victim is me,
His horn cuts the air just inches from my knee!
Violently I jump to the side I go,
Adrenaline comes forth, I escape my foe!

I have done two safaris in my life,
My first and my last, I want no strife!
If animals you love, no danger you fear,
Africa's a wonder, you'll hold it near!!

Church Camp

It's a church group that's about to board.
We're off to Wyoming to worship the Lord.

It's a five day camp that awaits us there.
These youth will spend some time in prayer.

Let's give these kids and their leaders a hand,
They are the backbone of our land.

As this bus carries them back to their home,
May God be with them wherever they roam!

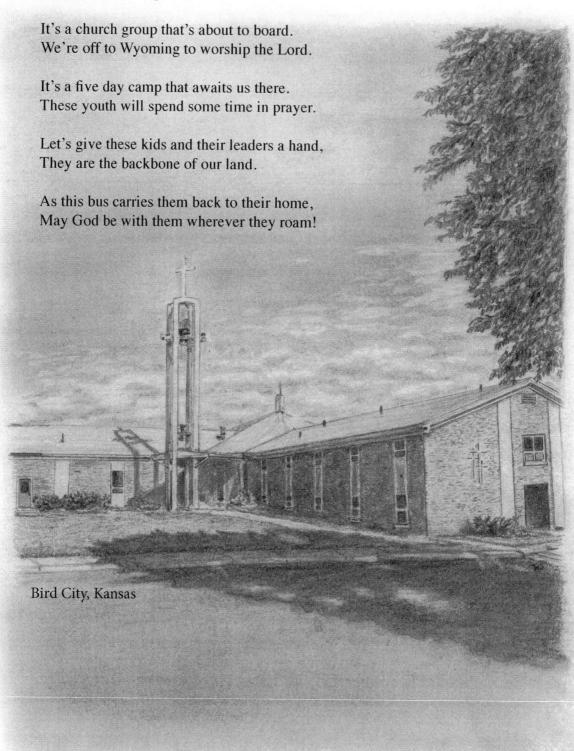

Bird City, Kansas

The Sun Talks to the Earth

I am the SUN warming your day.
Projecting a beam till you catch the ray.

I observe you spinning so dizzy I think,
Below your horizon each day I do sink!

Close to the surface my violence portrayed,
This rebel behavior, to you seem delayed!

A foe I can do, usually friendly I am,
Basking with me is like cuddling a lamb!

So sorry dear sir, I warn you Mister,
When I turn up the heat, imagine a blister!

As you run away, I am pulling you in,
Like a spoiled child, where have you been?

I hold you close, you depend on my heat,
When you're out on the beach my touch you meet.

As your moods do change, I affect you all,
But I enjoy you most blue beautiful ball!

The Farmer & His Daughter

In the field her father was spending much of his time.
Five point pitch in the pool hall, he'd play with only a dime.

The art of farming, it's a creative art,
Intricate in nature and luck is a part.

Two factors we speak, weather and price, important to succeed,
But to this man dedication the key, as he plants a tiny seed!

This way of living, disappoints are many, tenacity the spice of life,
Character it builds, children grow up, environment for man and wife.

Two years of work, we wait for the crop,
It's wheat we want, don't let the price drop!

The Noah and Pearl Leach barn, built in 1916 in Bird City, Kansas.
Eight feet was cut off the base, and this is only the haymow.

The weather threatens; there are thousands at stake,
Just hours to go and the combines will take,

Those bountiful bushels to the harvest bin!
Don't count your money, it's a curse times ten!

A hail storm comes through, huge chunks of ice,
The crop is wiped out, sadly missed this price!

An enormous loss, tremendous defeat, we must face our fears,
The farmer's daughter observes her father, her eyes are filled with tears!

No sleep for this man, the night of the storm, he knows the banker does see,
Cash flow must work, credit is tight, the storm brings the farmer to his knee.

He contemplates this crisis, many years of experience he owns,
The banker will wait, his credit's still good, next year pay down on his loans.

These wonderful people our farmers, they continue when times get tough,
The children surmount their problems when others have had enough!

Many years on a tractor across a field going forth and back,
Large estates sometimes are built, by the ones who have the knack!

The farmer's daughter, a lovely girl, raised with an ethic of work,
Moved to the city, education she did, her childhood a definite perk!

Her peers in the city, she often watched, surprised at times you can bet,
Because the background she had, from the farm indeed, she would never forget!

The "Charging Bull" sculpture in the financial district of New York City.

Stock Market Savvy

Fascinating it is, the stock market, today,
Shall we buy, shall we sell, please show us the way!

Adrenaline oh yes, take my pulse do check,
If you think you predict, just prepare for a wreck!

Fortunes are made over time and lost,
A very fun hobby, at times quite a cost!

Television we watch for hints and advice,
Often they're right, step back roll the dice.

A sixth sense, some people possess,
Others crash and burn, not pleasant oh yes!

So rewarding it is, when the bull reigns the week,
Exactly the opposite, with the bear so bleak.

Nasdaq, the DOW, S&P, what a show!
Don't risk what you can't, just collect the dough!

How can a stock go from three to thirty times?
Money to be made, millions down to dimes.

Some advice they say, long term just hold,
The advisers, not their money, of course they're bold!

It's fun to observe, some call it a game,
With your wisdom, invest, you may obtain fame!

Check Out Girl

Her face was red, by the register she stood,
The eyes they were bloodshot, were her children in the hood?

My cart is quite full, she is checking me through,
Is it alcohol or depression, I wish that I knew.

"Your Christmas, how was it?" This question I asked.
Her response, I can sense many problems she amassed.

"I was alone," she shrugged, "My husband's in jail,"
"Haven't talked to my children!" Through my heart stabs a nail.

"Hang in there, girl, things have to improve."
The interest I have, her expression does move.

A smile it is forming, even laughter comes through,
Her excitement, so contagious, yes happy me too!

A gift my lady, a small tip I do share,
This token of friendship, for you I do care.

Foolishly spend this money tonight,
You need a break, a reward with delight!

Her mood is now changed, a smile on her face,
We can't stop now, just dress her in lace!

Tomorrow now displays, her job returns,
Last night so crazy, but for it she yearns!

Short break from a life that some call mundane,
An escape from the strife, an escape from the pain!

The world marches on, we continue at this pace,
We're in it together, we are the human race!

Antarctica Bound

Antarctica our goal, a storm will ascend,
Let's start at the first and not at the end!

Janeiro to begin, Copacabana the beach,
The ladies in thongs are beyond my reach!

This beach in Brazil, fantastic I'm glad,
Thousands of bodies just sparsely clad.

From Kansas I am, no water around,
This beach in Brazil, fun I have found!

Iguazu, the waterfall we will,
It's on the border, Argentine and Brazil.

This is one of three top in the world,
It's a project I say that God unfurled!

Montevideo, Uruguay we say,
Most stable of all, country okay!

Buenos Aires, Tango let's dance,
Eva Perón, she took a stance.

From humble beginnings, she controlled the land,
Her sexual allure brought a sensual command.

The people loved her, for them she stood,
Her power reached for the people's good!

The Falkland Islands we're talking about,
The penguins are huge, I brag if you doubt!

Ushuaia, Argentina, Patagonia southern tip,
Bitter cold in winter, whiskey let us sip!

Antarctica ahead, we dodge big chunks of ice,
To hit a berg as large as these, our ship would pay the price!

Our destination finally reached, the Captain starts to talk,
Uneasy weather coming, our ship the storm does stalk!

We must leave early, starting now, danger on our heel,
Waves are tall against our glass, captain takes the wheel!

Largest waves in the world, are at the Cape Horn tip,
Captain tucks us in a cove, on this ship he has a grip!

Twelve, hours we do sit, our anchor is fully out,
This man in charge, has the skill, we know without a doubt!

The storm is gone, anchor up, we shoot around the horn,
Sailing north, observe the ice, Chilean glaciers here are born!

From Santiago we fly home, but first two days of fun,
A rodeo, sombreros fly, the cowboys are on the run!

From this city in Chile, comes copper from the mine,
From their vineyards and bottles, the tempting taste of wine!

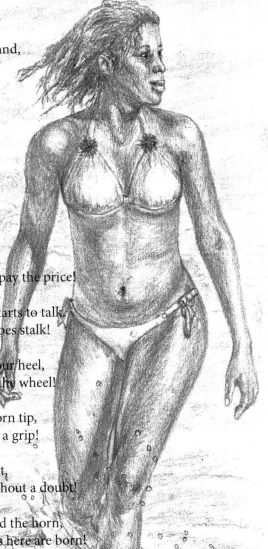

Antarctica

100 Cities Around the World

New York, New York, Statue of Liberty does prevail,
Times Square and Broadway, new Freedom Tower we hail!

Champs-Élysées in Paris, Moulin Rouge and Crazy Horse,
Most visited attraction in the world, the Eiffel Tower of course!

From New Delhi, India to the Taj Mahal, roundtrip in only a day,
The Gateway to India in Mumbai, an historic site I will say!

Rio de Janeiro, in Brazil let's just hang out,
Copacabana Beach, watching people as we walk about!

Christ the Redeemer, new wonder of the world,
On the mountain in Rio, what a site unfurled!

Argentina is so close, Buenos Aires is our stop,
Tango the favorite dance, Eva Perón is the top!

Twenty five million, Seoul, South Korea, many people here,
Beautiful view from the Seoul Tower on a day that's clear!

Beijing, China has The Great Wall, also Tiananmen Square,
Cairo, Egypt the Pyramids and artifacts we know are rare!

Our flight lands in Rome, it's Italy to behold,
The Vatican is impressive, the Colosseum so bold!

The Autostrada a car we rent, to lovely Florence we drive,
Botticelli's "Birth of Venus", the Uffizi we arrive!

Venice is our next stop, the canals we love to see,
On a water taxi we embark, to St. Mark's are we.

Tokyo, Japan, a magnificent city we like to enjoy,
Mount Fuji is our goal today, our guide is just a boy!

Don't leave Japan, so clean it is we still have much to do,
Sumo Wrestling is number one, through the streets our taxi flew!

London is next, Big Ben we know, Diana we miss so much,
To Amsterdam on a high speed train, now we visit the Dutch!

Prostitution is legal, pot is smoked and windmills do exist,
The Netherlands it is and Holland it's called, this country some have missed!

Turkey right now, our ship does dock, Istanbul so fun,
The Blue Mosque, so intriguing it is, reflecting in the sun!

The Grand Bazaar, three thousand shops, the biggest enclosed mall,
Sixteen million, the people here, three thousand mosques in all.

In Greece it stands, up so high on top of the Acropolis,
It's the Parthenon in Athens, standing in awe are us!

United Arab Emirates, Dubai is the city for now,
The tallest building in the world, impressive let's take a bow!!

Table Mountain, enjoying the view from the top,
South Africa, it's Cape Town, in a taxi we hop.

Cape Town, our favorite, such a tantalizing tour,
So friendly they are while drinking the best liqueur.

Hong Kong metropolitan, China comes to mind,
A favorite for me, just let your body unwind.

Macau so close, the new Las Vegas of Asia,
Kuala Lumpur, twin towers in Malaysia.

Denver, Colorado, the capitol is a mile high,
Marijuana is sold there, a very cheap way to fly!

San Antonio, Texas, brave men at the Alamo,
Crockett, Bowie and more, they all died a hero!

North we go to Alaska, Anchorage and Fairbanks,
Much interest in the Iditarod, very high it ranks.

Toronto is in Canada, the people here are many,
Ride their tower to the top, just go and spend your penny.

Lazola, in Cape Town

"Here's lookin at you kid!" We're now in Casablanca,
Drink coffee in Morocco, espresso please, not Sanka!

In Spain we are, and the capital city is Madrid,
Tapas bars are fun, the Prada Art Museum we did.

The city now is Moscow, we have traveled really quite far,
Beautiful domes in Russia, famous vodka at the bar!

Bangkok, Thailand, definitely an interesting place,
A ten dollar massage, or the palace with a gold face.

Australia now it is, in Sydney let's make a stop,
The world famous Opera House, ranks right at the top.

Buy a ticket let's catch a flight, Ayres Rock is now our goal,
This rock is huge, color is red, travel's so fun, we're on a roll.

Ushuaia, Argentina, oh yes the southern tip,
It's Patagonia, South America, sign up and take the trip.

A rodeo in Chile, Santiago is the spot,
Front row we hope to get, our tickets we have bought.

It's Reykjavik in Iceland, the Blue Lagoon it's always warm,
Huge waterfalls are near this place, scholastics are the norm!

San Francisco Golden Gate, intriguing beauty of this bridge,
Richmond in Virginia, located near the Blue Ridge.

Cusco in Peru, gasp for air as you sleep all night,
Machu Picchu very close, to climb so high use all your might.

Experience the beauty of Chicago, skyscrapers on a lake,
Collins Avenue, Miami Beach, careful now your skin will bake.

In Germany, Baden-Baden, nude bathing close your eyes,
Munich and Frankfurt, thriving cities as we said good byes.

Belfast in Northern Ireland, it's where the Titanic was built,
Glasgow is in Scotland, you might be dressed in a kilt.

Most western point in Europe, it's Lisbon, Portugal,
Helsinki, Finland, we do have lunch, our stomachs now are full.

Manneken Pis, in Brussels, Belgium, little boy saved the day,
Zurich, Switzerland, army knife, just how much will you pay?
(continued)

The Little Mermaid, a hundred years, Copenhagen, Denmark,
Stockholm, Sweden, Nobel the Prize, visit their lovely park.

Acapulco, Mexico, the cliff divers you have to see,
California, LA it is, massive city spreads to the sea.

Wichita in Kansas, airplane capital, the world around,
A city we love is Houston, Texas we are bound.

Panama City on the canal, go through the locks you must,
Ottawa, Canada, capital it is, we're filled with wanderlust.

Bird City, in Kansas, tractors are farming corn and wheat,
Boston, Mass, the North Church, this tour we cannot beat.

Belize City, Caribbean, the climate here is so nice,
Montego Bay, Jamaica, the night life sí, is full of spice!

Budapest, Hungary, split on the Danube River,
Tallinn in Estonia, will be our next endeavor.

Up the Amazon River, our ship goes eight, hundred miles,
The exciting city of Manaus, Brazil, faces are all smiles.

Papeete, Tahiti, in the middle of the Pacific Ocean,
Very expensive here, bring plenty of suntan lotion.

On the equator in Ecuador, it is the city of Quito,
An educational experience, please just have a burrito.

Nha Trang in Vietnam, motor scooters and low prices,
Cochin is in India, many stores and shops for spices.

The capital city is Berlin, also Brandenburg Gate,
Stone Mountain in Atlanta, get there early, don't be late.

Second largest building in the world, Romania, Bucharest,
Warsaw, Poland is in Europe, it is one of the best.

Lima, Peru, it's on the coast, please bring me a Pisco Sour.
Pisco, also Peru, we'll drink for another hour!

Grafton Street, Dublin, Ireland, it is Molly Malone,
The Tart with a Cart, make a call just use your phone.

Norway, it's Oslo, visit the Viking Ship Museum,
Prague the city of beauty, a real European gem.

Muscat, Oman, if your car is not clean, a fine you receive,
Christ Church in New Zealand, sheep shearing, it's wool we weave.

Stanley in the Falkland Islands, penguins are everywhere,
Largest statue in Dakar, Senegal, site is very rare.

Basilica Familia, number one, in Barcelona, Spain,
Cardiff, Wales, grab an umbrella and visit their castle in the rain,

Waikiki, it's Honolulu, the capital of Hawaii,
From here, we call home, our cell phones work for free.

Bergen, Norway, Geirangerfjord, what a view to behold,
Lipizzaner Stallions, Vienna, Austria, they are so very bold.

The currency in Vietnam, Ho Chi Minh, we say Saigon,
It's spelled dong, pronounced dung, watch before your money's gone.

A half a million dong equals U.S. dollars, twenty four.
A half million bill, quite impressive, please open door.

St. Petersburg, Russia, Church of the Spilled Blood,
Ephesus, Turkey, the home of Mary, not the big flood,

Sky Tower, Auckland, New Zealand, elevate to the top,
Notre Dame Basilica, French Montreal, please do stop.

Fairmont Le Chateau, Quebec City, a Canadian jewel,
Las Vegas, Nevada, just roll the dice and enter the pool.

The Brisbane River meanders through town, Australia at its best,
The countryside, sunshine and hills, these people do have zest!

Jeepneys in Manila, the Philippines let us cheer,
The nightclubs line Malate, great dancing we do hear.

On the Black Sea is Varna, the water is really quite dark,
Some girls on the beach are topless, an umbrella you can park.

Hobart's in Tasmania, the little Devil, you can see here,
Kotor, Montenegro, on the Adriatic, we do cheer.

A boat to Indonesia, Batam so close to Singapore,
Fantastic mall Batam does have, your credit card might soar.

These are a hundred cities, we could go on and on,
We have to stop somewhere, bright clothing we do don!

It's a Conundrum to Me

Whatever happened, it's a conundrum to me,
The body, how awful, for the world to see.

Did she fall, was she pushed, will that cable hold?
Dear God, get her down, those men are so bold.

The bridge, quite large and powerful alone,
But this tragedy, this fall, she's cut to the bone!

Don't think it's suicide, did the wind blow her there?
This is big, it's news, she's the daughter of our mayor!

She was dating this man, a broker who trades,
Quite wealthy I hear, and my memory fades.

Oh yes I recall, fancy cars the man does,
Can anyone tell where tonight he was?

His Lamborghini seen, on the east side bypass,
His tires were spinning, his foot, on the gas.

No way, this can't be, she is down and alive?
The message laid out on TV it's live!

How critical this girl, it's got to be bad,
On TV we observe, here comes her Dad.

Distraught his face, as he rushes the door,
His daughter near death, his emotions do soar!

Everywhere roadblocks, sports car will be found,
Authority on the streets, tonight they do abound.

The girl is coming to, the truth will soon be told,
Pushed the girl he did, this man his soul he sold.

An all points bulletin for the man they do chase,
No mercy will be shown, it's a murder attempt case.

Bulletin now just coming in, info we do lack,
Read you now loud and clear, sports car on its back!

Ambulance Emergency

The ambulance rolled out, the weather is brisk,
Black ice disregard, we'll take the risk!

Collision head on, Holy God let us pray,
Our pulse is racing, with adrenaline we'll pay!

Organize, think ahead, prepare, we arrive.
Two figures on the pavement appearing not to be alive!

Only three of us for now, more people here soon,
One car in the water, how deep is that lagoon?

Triage those two, I'll wade out to the car,
They're depending on us, EMT's we are.

The car in the water, the top is sticking out.
Reaching in the water, I am scared without a doubt!

No bodies I feel, no legs, not an arm,
The occupants of the vehicle live a life of charm!

Another ambulance, more help is now here,
That other car, has been slammed in the rear!

Bring C-collars, spine boards and oxygen fast,
Let's hurry with this one, I'm afraid he won't last!

Look under this car, a person might be,
Lift up the auto, ten men are the key!

Thank you guys, we are satisfied now,
This car landing here, we do not know how!

It's a tension pneumothorax, get her on the way,
Keep the hammer down, speeding as you pray!!

Bring the jaws of life, his knee is under the dash,
He's in a lot of pain, it's been a hell of a crash!

It's the third ambulance coming to the scene,
Our last injured patient is only a teen!

Thank you to the Firemen and the Highway Patrol,
We work as a team, we're always ready to roll!

Jim's Bus Driver Safety Speech

It's a safety speech I give you now,
An emergency could happen and only how!

To alarm you unduly is not my goal,
Safety is our motto, it's a bus drivers' role.

The windows are exits, pull out on the bar,
Push out at the bottom and head for afar!

There are two exits in the top of the bus,
At the front and the back it's better for us.

Be careful in the aisle, I may hit the brakes.
You'll go through the windshield and be hurt for Pete's sake!

A fire extinguisher there is, it's under this seat,
Hand it to the driver so he can tackle the heat.

The seats do recline, but don't you forget,
Hot coffee can burn and this you can bet!

The armrests fold up, the footrests go down,
It's somewhat confusing, don't give me that frown!

This ends my safety poem for the day,
Let's get on the road and we'll be on our way!

The Old Indian Senses Danger

After wearily ascending to the pinnacle, the old warrior balanced unsteadily on the jagged rock of a magnificent bluff, and his aging but alert eyes scanned the vast prairie that engulfed the view to the horizon. Inhaling a powerful surge of crisp, spring air, Grey Wolf was invigorated with memories from a lifetime of challenging accomplishments, and these euphoric feelings were enhanced; because even today, standing precariously on the granite pedestal high above the bountiful plains, he still possessed the ambition and desires of his youth.

His leathery skin, toughened by the wind and dried by the sun, had experienced the severity of many winters and summers. Grey Wolf's body was lean, muscled from years of fighting and hunting, and though surrounded with abundance, he lived in a savage era laced with obtrusions of danger. His vision was not what it once had been, but the beauty of the picture before him quickened his pulse and a tingling sensation of pride rippled up his spine and intruded to the depths of his soul.

The great buffalo were there before him. With rugged perseverance, they had escaped the attrition of time, as had the Indians who hunted them. Providing their pursuers with a lifeline of sustenance, the majestic beasts were infinite in number and existed as immense dark islands in a sea of lush grass. The fifteen to thirty buffalo hides needed to cover a teepee would shelter a family from unpredictable climatic changes. Even though the crafty Indians hunted deer, beaver, rabbits, geese, and other game, the meat from the splendid buffalo, dried in the sun to make jerky, was their greatest source of nourishment. The intriguing Buffalo Dance gave inspiration and assurance for a successful hunt. The goodness and greatness of this land and these laws of living extended into the spiritual and would last for eternity.

"He could move silently like a gentle breeze and with the stealth of a spirit. His physical appearance revealed marks of bravery, old wounds were healed, leaving deep scars of courage."

Colored with war paint and shielded by his guardian spirit, Grey Wolf had scalped many of the enemy. The warring between tribes was a saga as ancient as the Indians themselves. The old warrior's wisdom spanned decades of mastering the art of fighting, and he was often chosen as the bravest man to lead his people into fierce battle. Accepting many Honor Feathers for his fearless acts, his skills of tracking and hunting were deeply respected by brothers of his race; he could move silently like a gentle breeze and

with the stealth of a spirit. His physical appearance revealed marks of bravery, old wounds were healed, leaving deep scars of courage.

Grey Wolf's sons had become great fighters in their own right, taught by a sagacious father who knew the laws of survival, as only the experience of time could unfold. The greatness of the Indian and the control of his surroundings were unparalleled, as Grey Wolf felt the exhilaration created by dominion.

Puffs of thick smoke signaled danger as a speck in the distance slowly magnified into the clear picture of a man on a horse. With increasing interest, the trained eyes of Grey Wolf noticed the steady, determined advance of this lonely rider. The approaching threat was unlike any warrior Grey Wolf had fought. The man did not sit directly on the horse, but on a piece of leather; he had peculiar clothing covering his body and head. There was no bow or arrow; there was no spear or war paint. Turning from these thoughts, the chilling fact that brought anxiety and even fear to Grey Wolf's mind was the color of the man's skin. It was pale, almost white. Grey Wolf observed and pondered the future.

Our Journey Soon Ends

Our journey soon ends,
But thank you my friends,

For your kindness and fun,
Through each day's run.

An empty bus is quiet indeed.
It needs lovely people to take the lead,

To tour the mountains and the countryside,
To see the cities with a step on guide.

Coast to coast and border to border,
This magnificent land seems to be in order.

The rivers, the oceans, the clouds above,
They're all painted with God's love.

As we close for the day, the sun will dim,
I say bye for now, your bus driver Jim.

It's a Motor Coach

It's a motor coach they sometimes say,
It runs down the road day after day.
Does charter work, tours and the like,
Many times driving on the smooth turnpike.

Forty five feet is the length.
The frame you know has lots of strength.
The wheels are big, the tires are sound.
Mile after mile they follow the ground.

Five hundred horses lined up in a row,
But it's really the customer that makes the bus go.
It takes money to make, big machines work,
If it's not coming in, chaos will lurk.

A motor coach tour is a thing of beauty,
The driver and the escort are doing their duty.
The sights, the smells, the sounds on the road,
The colors, the diesel, the noise from your load.

The mountains, they're tall, the brakes must not fail.
If the driver is careless he'll end up in jail.
But we as drivers are a responsible lot.
We prove ourselves or they want us not.

The new trips are out, they're calling you.
Pick one out, you can join us too!
Your reward will be great, this we know.
You'll love our trips, so come on and go!

The Night Is Twisted

The night is twisted, a maze of puzzles, intricately interwoven, merging like memories of a lifetime, forming a blur as tears flow across my pupils. Thoughts enter my mind like rapid fire shots from a machine gun piercing the cerebrum from every direction. The intensity builds, confusion intertwined with facets of clear thought.

I have to do something, am sure I just witnessed a murder, but is the man really dead? That lady is running away with the killer. They both look directly into my eyes. Her red blouse projects boldness as they disappear down the dirty subway steps. The shooter used a silencer, because he pointed the gun and the victim fell, but there was no sound. My chest, cringes with anxiety, as cold drops of sweat saturate my forehead. Why did I come to this city? Don't get involved; it is only trouble. A nagging feeling of guilt tugs at my childhood rules. Fear grips my soul! I cannot let this pass; the police must be notified. My thumb and forefinger slide my smart phone from my front pocket and I enter the pin. Oh no, they have returned. The red blouse and the man in the dark suit are approaching me. I see the gun and jump to the left as the first bullet pierces my right shoulder. My white sport coat absorbs the bright crimson blood as the second hollow point explodes into my chest. I am collapsing and darkness overcomes my body.

Walk to the Edge

Board this bus and travel with me,
Pick your tour and the world you can see.

Escape with us from your mundane life,
Walk to the edge of the razor sharp knife.

Experience you seek, thrills you will find,
Just come with me, let your body unwind.

Sometimes let me say life is too cold,
Loosen up, relax, go for the gold.

Many places out there are calling you,
Unusual, exciting, there are things to do.

I invite you, mount up, ride to the edge.
Peek over out there, just beyond the ledge.

Don't stay home as the world goes by,
Let's see these places before we die.

In the nude, on the equator, sunburn we had,
Oh my this is travel, it wasn't that bad.

Fat Tuesday, Mardi Gras, Bourbon Street oh well,
The things we saw that day, don't tell.

London, Hong Kong and Paris for a start,
Istanbul to Cape Town, these places you will dart!

Motor coach, cruise ship, airline take your pick,
Around the world do all three, out your neck you will stick!

Antarctica and around Cape Horn, icebergs big as ships,
Roughest water in the world, hang on for tidal rips.

Machine guns in the world, don't get nervous, they are there,
Wilderness walks in Alaska, don't be challenged by a bear.

Pirates lurk on the seas, if we're boarded we are stuck,
Lions attack in the wild, puncture tires on the truck.

Pickpockets everywhere, hold your purse, keep it tight,
Take a break, get some rest, drink a beer that is light.

Street savvy when you're followed, step aside, let them pass.
Obey the rules in each country, out of jail, don't harass.

Istanbul and Athens, two great markets when you shop,
Get online, buy your ticket, travel the world and don't stop!

Homesick Cruise Ship Girl

"Are you married," I said, "Children?" I asked.
"No," to one question, her smile is a mask!

"So lucky" I say, "Much money you save,
Cruising the world, it is all the rave."

"Your job on the ship, experiences you've had,
The envy of many, but you seem so sad?"

Her mind is far off, as the words come out,
The eyes start to sparkle and they dance about.

"It's marriage I seek, a family to raise.
A dress for my wedding, it's all the craze!"

"Flowers of beauty, romance in the air,
It's every girl's dream; it's every girl's prayer."

Such a lovely person, determined she is,
From Lima, Peru she still is a miz.

So young we know, many years are ahead,
No hurry girl, to the man you will wed.

"If I see you no more, have a great life,"
To the lucky man, what a fabulous wife!

A Tribute to My Friends

My Friend - Stunt Pilot!

The people, the names, the events—it all happened and is recorded here as accurately as I remember. Bob Bressler was born February the second on Ground Hog's Day. Because of this fact, we enjoy watching each year to see if the furry little woodchuck pops out of his earthen "Home on the Range," to spot his shadow.

My buddy Bob, one might say, grew up in an airplane cockpit. His father Ernie Bressler piloted a plane before him. In the early fifties, when most people were flying kites, Ernie and his wife Hope, flew their little Cessna from a small rural area in Kansas to Manhattan Island, over the Empire State Building, landing at LaGuardia International Airport and continuing by taxi to Macy's to do, what else, but their Christmas shopping. I still own a precision built toy car, with a horn and controlled steering that was a gift from that trip. Bob picked the car that had the gear shift in it. Ernie started the forerunner of Flight for Life, in our small community. He would fly numerous medical emergencies to Denver and Colorado Springs, day or night, in a 170 Cessna. Eventually he owned a 185 Cessna which came out with a cargo door which was perfect for loading a gurney on the aircraft. The man joined the Civil Air Patrol. He organized spotters for the Ground Observer Corps (GOC), which they started under the Eisenhower administration to cover blank spots in our radar system and to help facilitate national security. Bob and I would study the black airplane silhouettes in the booklet sent out by the Air Force. We nervously thought of spotting a Russian bomber

and saving our country from annihilation. When Christmas came, Santa Claus circled our town in an airplane flown by Ernie, dropping small sacks of candy to happily screaming children, who had not heard of the slower, less efficient sleigh and reindeer. I can still hear the drone of the engine and see Santa's smiling face as bags of candy hit the pavement. Some of them would break into smithereens, sending peanut clusters, cherry chocolates, Tootsie Rolls and hard candy bouncing and dodging each other until competitive child hands scooped them up.

As excited as a youngster can become, we would holler until our vocal chords were numb, "Get ready, get ready; here he comes again!" I know that Norm Dorsch would often fill in when Santa was too busy to be there for the day!!

This was to become a family of aviators; flying farmers, they called them. Hope, Bob's mother, soloed in the Cessna herself. She even had red airplanes inlaid into her grey kitchen linoleum, an incredulous feat to an eight-year-old observer.

I first saw Bob Bressler near the center of town by his Dad's store, Bressler Imple-

"He would fly numerous medical emergencies to Denver and Colorado Springs, day or night, in a 170 Cessna."

ment, when we were small children and observed from across the street an active boy with obvious confidence. I, the cautious, take life seriously type, felt intimidated by his eyes squinting at me, as though he was looking into the bright Kansas sun. At the age of four that kid obviously knew things I did not and am sure he had already been around the block a few times, probably by himself. I noticed Bob from time to time in our thriving metropolis of five hundred people, but didn't meet him until first grade where we formed a bond of friendship that would last for more than forty years.

> *"I, the cautious, take life seriously type, felt intimidated by his eyes squinting at me, as though he was looking into the bright Kansas sun."*

Sometime in the fourth grade Bob came up with his famous over used question, "Is that all?" It didn't matter how magnificent one's story would be, his only reply was, "Is that all?"

I told him my Dad's '53 Ford would run eighty and you're right; that's exactly what he said. Believe me; impressing Bob in the fourth grade was difficult!

The incorrigible, bright, happy little child did everything, everywhere, all the time! One day I invited him down to my Dad's farm repair shop to mess around and have some fun.

Messing around to Bob was standing on a table saw with his foot two inches from the blade, reaching high enough to plug the motor in and then listening to my father frantically plead at a volume higher than the spinning saw, "Robert, Robert, stay there! Don't move!"

Dad quickly ran to the saw, lifted Robert straight up, away from the blade. He set the petrified child firmly on the concrete floor and reached up and unplugged the menacing, noisy foot cutter-offer. Sometimes when I think I'm becoming forgetful, my mind is amazed at its vivid recall of a situation that happened so many years ago. It's as clear to me as if it happened this morning.

At an early age, Bob developed a temper he later outgrew, but until he did, his demeanor sometimes entertained us. One afternoon we were playing down on the old lot, where Skeet Underwood later built a new home. Bressler got all worked up about something, and he jumped on his bicycle and headed for the side of a nearby garage, which was newly covered with white siding. He gained speed rapidly and he bawled and screamed loud enough to keep three of us curiously concerned about the inevitable. He must have been going ten or fifteen miles per hour when at the last second he bailed off and the bicycle impacted against the building with enough force to bring us all running to investigate the obliterated machine. No kidding, Bob didn't put a scratch on that bike, nor did he bend the front wheel. We could see a smudgy tire (continued) print on the white building and we examined it carefully. Soon everyone slapped their legs and laughed, including Bob. I sometimes envied his quick change fun personality.

They called the popular game we played on the corner lot "Five Hundred." A player had to catch enough balls from the batter to win. A fly ball is worth a hundred, a one bouncer is worth fifty, a two bouncer is twenty-five, and if one snags a grounder, a minuscule five. When Bob would win with five hundred, I would only have sixty-five, maybe a one bouncer and three grounders. He would usually figure out some excuse to let me bat though I never won. Bressler threw a baseball twice as far as any of his peers. Once near Enders Dam, I saw him skip a flat rock three splashes across the water. Try that sometime. When my friend would use that muscular arm and his first baseman's glove, the only first baseman's glove I'd ever seen at that age, he did impress me. The rest of us had regular old baseball gloves. Bressler often looked at them as if he thought they were below his skill level, ha!

Bob started to build his physique and throwing arm in third grade by putting cinnamon rolls on his Mom's charge account at "Bake Smith's Bakery." Bake added to several waistlines around town with his famous crispy recipe and they still closely guard the secret formula fifty years later. If you would have asked the late Uke Lillich, and if you were lucky enough she might have had a plate full of them on her counter. Bake didn't have to advertise because the pleasant smells from his shop filled the whole downtown area. People would try to head for the post office but when they started to pass his door their bodies automatically turned into the aroma.

Hope and Ernie, avid Carry Nation supporters, brought some tequila back from Mexico, probably to demonstrate its toxicity. Bob and I took this powerful concoction down to his basement and he poured some into a jar lid. He struck a match, lighting the alcohol, and I admired his unquestionable knowledge.

"Hope and Ernie, avid Carrie Nation supporters, brought some tequila back from Mexico, probably to demonstrate its toxicity."

Scowling, he groaned, "Can anyone imagine drinking that stuff? A person can probably get inebriated from the fumes!"

Inebriated was one of those colossal words Bob picked up when he was little, probably from Hope's reading to him! We both felt unquestionably, the tequila would eat one's esophagus up before it could reach the stomach. Bob and I could see a worm in the bottom of the bottle, which added to the mystique of this strange product from "Old Mexico."

We boys would happily sit on each side of Hope on that enormous soft couch they had in their home and she would read to us. My friend did not apply himself in school as much as he could have, but because of Hope's reading and his high IQ, he would later in life, slaughter us at Trivial Pursuit. He knew things like the difference between a dromedary and a camel. Bob was a people charmer and we loved to have him in our home.

He once inquired of my Mother, Ruth, "Does anyone ever call you "ruthless?" Heck, we call my Mom "hopeless" all the time."

This boy enjoyed his childhood. It was Tonka truck mania on his dirt pile and Lionel train infatuation down at the Bressler Implement Christmas display, a Massey Harris Dealership. I delivered papers for the McCook Gazette and the papers were dropped daily to me by a pilot in a Cessna airplane. Of course this fascinated the future pilot and he liked to come down with me to my Dad's lot where we would wait for the plane. The Gazette flyer would come in low, like a crop duster, and we would try to catch the bundle, or at least imitate a catcher. Nevertheless, we always chickened out at the last second because the papers were dangerous traveling at that speed.

> "Does anyone ever call you "ruthless?" Heck, we call my Mom "hopeless" all the time."

I mowed the high school lawn for a few years. Once Robert and I got up at four o'clock in the morning and headed for the school with our matching Moz All lawn mowers. We mounted flash lights on the decks and mowed in the dark,

pretending we were the Lindstens, who were big farmers that ran three tractors in the same field.

Bressler and I liked to stop at his grandmother Addie Bressler's when I delivered her paper. She put us in two chairs at her table and then split an orange for our snack. We could never coax her into getting the salt and pepper collection out of the curved glass case for us to play with. We thought her to be a wonderful lady, but she became quite obstinate on that one point. Hope's daughter Shryll still displays this collection yearly at the Bird City Steam Engine Show.

We made X-shaped boomerangs in Cub Scouts, and once we, including Mike Burr and Kent Chapman, fought with BB guns at night. Someone hit Rex, Bob's brother, in the side of the head, just above his ear with a BB. It's a wonder some kid didn't lose an eye that night. Four or five of us got into the tunnel digging mood. We made the vacant lot beside our house look like a drunken, back hoe operator had been on the loose. Bill Elliott, who would later become an electrical engineer, wired the tunnels with lights. My Dad got so upset with the looks of his lot, and the neighbors driving by shaking their heads, he made us cover it up. Funny thing, there weren't nearly as many cover uppers as there were diggers.

With about twenty mischievous kids in the back of a farm truck, Bressler and I went on a Boy Scout trip to the mountains with Leonard and Melvin Mast as sponsors. Bob and I weren't ornery, but the other twenty boys were, ha! (cont'd)

"BOB

"*They say if one goes out in the late evening and walks on what is now named Bressler Street in Bird City, a far off sound projects from the heavens. It is not the "Spirit of St. Louis," because it is rumored only one angel is running a four cylinder, two hundred five horse Lycoming.*"

We did get out of hand once and got into a fight over---who can remember? He had a head lock on me from behind and his arm came right across my mouth. Although my parents taught me never to do such a thing, I bit him, and his reaction was not good. He squeezed all the harder, and I finally had to say uncle to breathe. He whipped me pretty darn good, but I forgot it within two hours. The sponsors allowed us to take only two and a half dollars spending money for the entire ten day trip. Someone wanted to play poker the second night out and Chuck Shull, who later became an airline pilot, lost two dollars of his money in one hand. He was one sick kid, knowing that fifty cents had to last the next eight days, but the rest of us were unmerciful and couldn't contain our laughter.

Talk about being terrified of snakes, Bob Bressler was. I had this Plaster of Paris rattlesnake my parents brought back from Arkansas, and Robert wouldn't stay all night at our house unless my mother hid the snake downstairs. Two other unpleasantries in his life were fried fish, fish of any kind for that matter, and coconut. My wife once tricked him by putting a plate of coconut cookies on the table. They weren't bad until he discovered a small shred of the white stuff and it about ruined his afternoon.

"Talk about being terrified of snakes, Bob Bressler was."

A '57 black and white Ford 300 found its way into Bob's life and he had Bette

Partch, a local artist, paint a "Running Bear" logo on each side of the car. Bressler would drag Bird Avenue with his windows down and the "Running Bear" song would blast away on his radio—"On the banks of the river stood a lovely Indian maid." The future aviator was a Ford man all the way, and I was die hard Chevy.

"Bob was one of God's finest productions. Maybe that's why my own son carries his name."

Naturally, Robert liked model airplanes and became quite proficient in the construction and the flying of the aircrafts. Albert Antholz helped Bob in learning the art of landing a model airplane. I marveled at Bob's ability to start an engine by cranking the propeller with his finger and not getting it severed. Most model airplane buffs carry nicks and wounds on their index or middle finger. The model airplane hobby followed him into his adult life, where radio controlled aircraft became "the thing."

Everyone loved Bob, but when his parents were upset with him they called him Robert Willard! His middle name was after Willard Moore, a man who was in the grain elevator business.

Bob was a farmer, licensed airplane mechanic, crop duster, stunt pilot, but first an outstanding leader in our church and community. This big happy Saint Bernard eagerly helped anyone he could. Bob was one of God's finest productions. Maybe that's why my own son carries his name.

My friend rebuilt a Piper Vagabond and he flew it over Lake Tahoe on the way to California. He fought prairie fires with his Piper Pawnee spray plane. The energetic pilot would practice dumping a full load of water on my farm, and I would take videos to help him improve his technique.

This pilot, dirt farmer, loved people, music, pepperoni pizza, and ketchup. The man with the appetite could tell one the location of any Pizza Hut within a three hundred mile radius. Bob was a World War II afficionado and he read books about airplanes, submarines and history. His favorite book was Jonathan Livingston Seagull, written by a pilot named Richard Bach. It is a wonderful story about a one in a million bird who loves to fly at high altitudes and do fantastic, high speed rolls and dives. The book teaches love of your fellowman, because Jonathan Livingston Seagull always looked for the good in everyone he met. Please read this book to fully understand this fabulous man we call Bob Bressler!!

"The energetic pilot would practice dumping a full load of water on my farm, and I would take videos to help him improve his technique."

Bob, and his partner Rod Young flew the planes they owned doing crop dusting. They often flew under the electric lines as they approached a field to get a better coverage on the crops! Their company name was Bressler Young Aviation and is still in business today.

Bob Bressler decided to build a stunt plane. With his partner Rod and many dedicated hours by both of these men, there emerged nine years, five thousand tiny nails, and seven coats of acrylic enamel later, a beautiful royal blue Pitts Special named "Rhapsody in Blue." The Pitts plane was a fantastic specimen with the cowling painted Corvette Red. It didn't surprise me that the airplane had the United Methodist insignia painted on one side of the tail and the Lutheran on the other side, the two churches that Bob and Rod attended. Bob's parents had seen that he attended Sunday school since he was baptized at two months old. Bob powered the plane with a four-cylinder Lycoming engine that developed 205 horsepower at 2,700 revolutions per minute. It had the stuff to make it go!

Rod Young, Albert Antholz, Jim, Cindy and a small group of admirers gathered for the first take off. Excited supporters cheered the sound of the thrilling, finely tuned engine, the sight of the spinning propeller in front of a beaming pilot, and the smell of fresh country air blurred with airplane exhaust fumes. The first flight filled us with admiration, excitement, relief and fear. In the weeks that followed, Bob practiced flying and I videoed his stunts. We would rush to the house to watch the tape and the next day he would improve the rolls, loops and hammerheads. He defined, with an effortless grin, that flying that Pitts was better than sex. I assume several stunt pilots might attest to that statement.

(continued)

On a bright Sunday morning in November, Bob, Willie Boyson and I sat in the local Dairy King discussing Charles Lindbergh, who lived in Bird City for three or four months in 1921. Willie was seven years old when he watched Lindbergh gather his parachute after making a jump one mile north of Bird City, Kansas.

Willie said, "Lindy was a tall, slender, quiet man and he didn't fly an airplane when he lived here. However, he wing walked and parachuted with another pilot flying the plane. Lindbergh did fly the "Spirit of St. Louis" over Bird City after his famous trans-Atlantic flight in 1927."

In fact, I had talked to Tom Sawyer that morning at the local "Rusty R" coffee shop and he said, "I was six years old and I sat on the football field when Lindy flew over. The town's people wrote "WELCOME" across the field with a human chain and Lindbergh circled five or six times acknowledging our enthusiasm. Yes, when one looks at the picture I am the small boy sitting on the ground because I got too tired standing."

> "Willie Boyson is no stranger to thrills and adventure and he probably should have worn the first "No Fear" t-shirt."

"Tom, how long did the people have to wait until Lindy flew over?"

"Oh, I suppose it was about forty-five minutes or so. We thought he'd land, but I guess he figured if the people mobbed him, he probably couldn't land his airplane safely and get it off the ground again."

The late Willie Boyson was no stranger to thrills and adventure and he probably should have worn the first "No Fear" t-shirt. When he was a young lad he stood on his head on top of the water tower for a quarter, promised to him by Gordon Weaver, an entrepreneur and large land baron. He later topped trees in the Northwest for a big lumber company, but his career ended when he fell more than a hundred feet before his gaff caught in the tree trunk. After they dropped the tree, his friend cut the spot out where his gaff stuck, saving his life. They sent this unusual piece of wood to him in the hospital and if one would have gone by his house sometime he would have drug it out. That Sunday morning, Bob, Willie and I sat talking in the Dairy King. I think Willie felt the aura of adventure that surrounded this daredevil wonderful friend we both had, and I also felt this nervous devotion as I was thinking of the dream I just had the night before of the day that was unfolding!! Deja Vu!!

It was this same Sunday on a beautiful afternoon when Bob was doing aerobatics near a farm owned by Rick and Linda Rogers. He went into a hammerhead and his little Pitts suddenly toppled over going into an inverted flat spin, turning counter clockwise as everything in the northern hemisphere turns. Rick and Linda were terrified as they watched the Pitts helplessly continue to spin and fall. Bob skillfully pulled the plane out of the spin, but he was too late. The beautiful "Rhapsody in Blue," with 5,000 tiny nails and seven coats of acrylic enamel, hit the ground and bounced, slamming into a mammoth four wheel drive John Deere tractor. Robert Willard crashed his airplane in farm country. He was dead!

"I choose to believe that a higher power, whom I call God, spared us from going on that run."

My wife and I were emergency medical technicians on the local ambulance. We had gone to a neighboring town, Colby, Kansas, to have dinner and were only ten minutes out of radio range when the call came in. I choose to believe that a higher power, whom I call God, spared us from going on that run.

We were sitting in a restaurant when our daughter called us. It was déjà vu for me. I had a premonition. Maybe others did too, as we watched him make his routine loops, barrel rolls, and hammerheads.

I felt my insides tear loose from where they were fastened. A silent wail pierced the air and no one heard. Tears meandered down these less than macho cheeks and an agonizing void that would take years in leaving, quickly filled my chest. My heart was ripped out and crushed between fear and disbelief. He was a friend, for a time that had just been determined, a friend with whom one could share his deepest secrets.

The funeral director said it was the biggest funeral the town had ever seen. Six hundred people attended in a town of four hundred. They did not come because he was a president or governor but because they loved him.

Jonathan Livingston Seagull plunged into the ground after a high speed dive and died, but soon found out he could go beyond death to a better world, continuing to help others. They say if one goes out in the late evening and walks on what is now named Bressler Street in Bird City, a person can see Jonathan Seagull diving through the clouds, or if one is especially quiet and listens, a far off sound projects from the heavens. It is not the "Spirit of St. Louis," because it is rumored only one angel is running a four cylinder, two hundred five horse Lycoming.

A Girl I Know

Her name is Cindy, she grew up on a farm.
She's a beautiful woman with talent and charm.

From pioneer stock her lineage is secure,
Tenacity and grit, they belong to her.

Work is her ethic, speed is her game.
A task completed, this is her aim.

She's fun, she's funny, she's contagious I say.
Besides her work, this girl likes to play!

Spontaneous, unpredictable, that's the way she was made,
Gorgeous and sexy, her youth does not fade.

At eight years old the girl drove a truck,
Hauling wheat to town, it was more than just luck.

Only girls in this family, no boys to work,
She was down in the grime and covered with murk.

The little girl drove a tractor, an adult she became.
With eyelashes and lipstick to the field she came.

Irrigation pipe was carried, she worked like a dog.
Nothing was beneath her, all the work she would hog.

It's a computer world now and here she thrives.
The keyboard is dancing as the stock market dives.

If her stocks were not sold, this we know,
It's not because the keys were moving too slow.

Constantly I chase her around the bedroom at night,
And also in the daytime, but she usually takes flight.

On occasion I catch her and this I know,
The wait is worth it when she does not say no!

(continued)

This beauty was prom queen a few years back,
It was obvious then she possessed the knack.

To accomplish goals she set out to do,
Perseverance and confidence, these are hers too.

Ten years on the ambulance as if spare time she had,
Many lives she has touched, these people are glad.

From a church, a community, a small town she came,
To the city where many would soon know her name.

High spirited for sure she never slows down,
We all know she has the best show in town.

Travel and tours are the agenda now.
Africa, Europe, and Asia, oh wow!

Her smile is beautiful and genuine indeed.
It draws you in, she takes the lead.

She's a scrapper like her daddy, she does pay her dues.
If you challenge her in battle, just prepare to lose!

As a child on the playground she could whip the boys.
You would hear them bawling, oh what a noise!

Flip the coin over only kindness is there,
Her body is full of love and of care.

Mama Cindy, her grandkids coined a term.
They're spoiled, she loves them and cannot be firm.

She waits on everyone within her reach,
Her time is divided and devoted to each.

We stand in line to receive our turn,
We bask in her praise and for it we yearn.

She's flying through life like a gold winged dove,
Every facet of this diamond I know and I love!

The Professional Lady

Gianna the girl, talented she is,
Clever and bright, the lady's a whiz!

She designs for us, and writes as well,
A tour book by her, our trips do sell!

So happy are we to discover such skill,
This girl does it all, she has the will!

Five years with us, dependable I say,
Photography plus acting, she does know the way!

Graphic design and computers indeed,
We'll stay with Gianna, she does take the lead!

Randy Ketzner the Builder

Randy Ketzner, he's a builder they say,
I'm talking houses, homes, day after day.

Thirty-eight years old, I call him a kid,
Eight hundred homes in Wichita he did.

How could a lad at this early age,
Accomplish so much, keep reading this page.

This man, I say boy because of my years,
Has drive, ambition, far above his peers!

Why do some men excel at this pace,
While others are spades, but just not the ace!

Who knows for sure, it's the genes we think,
This man is something, I write this in ink!

I decided in Wichita to have a home,
Who should build it, my mind starts to roam.

Bob Ketzner, I knew from my hometown,
Bird City, Kansas, write this name down.

Bob is Randy's dad, do you hear?
I told Randy step up, just give me your ear!

Randy I say, build a house just near,
Bird City blood in your veins, I must cheer!

This home he built is happiness to me,
It's gorgeous, I love it, come over and see!

A solid structure put together just right.
The floors, the walls, the seams are all tight.

Contractors, craftsmen, they all do appear.
Randy our man picks the best, don't fear!

They converged on our lot, ten at a time.
The back hoes, the loaders that turn on a dime.

Chaos it looked like, men everywhere,
These guys are tough, leathered skin they wear.

Manual labor we're talking, step up to the plate.
By muscle it's done, November's our date.

It's work it's sweat, determined these men.
Hammers, nails, shingles and tin.

This structure, it's form appeared quite fast.
I'm confident Randy, this home will last.

A salute to you and the men who were here,
Kick ass, my man it's you I cheer!

Randy Ketzner 1966 - 2014

Denelle Cuts My Hair

Denelle cuts my hair, stand back and look,
The phone rings now, the call she took.

Busy yes, the pulse of this shop,
Is racing, Denelle don't let the pace stop!

Sandy, Pam, Crystal, oh my,
These girls are cute, look through your eye.

Hair is flying, we see everywhere,
Colors like red, black, do we care?

Fix mine like that, the guy on the wall,
Young, good looking, he is quite tall.

Denelle I'm older, but magic you could,
Make me like him, oh please, you would.

Denelle's Shop, Wichita, Kansas

Thank you for trying, you talented girl,
You're great, it's good, you brought out my curl.

First, Class, Hair, they say,
Ambition Denelle, a price you will pay.

Hard work, dedication you know,
Denelle girl, I say just go.

This business will wear you down in time,
But honey who cares, I'll finish this rhyme.

To me you are a person so fine,
Come closer dear, pour a glass of wine.

This country was built by people like you,
Gritty, tenacious, a job you will do.

Day after day, yes year after year,
Some people work like you my dear.

I respect you, as a working mom,
My heart swells, and it seems to calm.

To know, you and your powerful drive,
A girl, a woman, who will survive!

The Wedding in Scotland

Marriage you say, what is the date?
Are you sure Janet, you've picked a mate?

Scotland, you're kidding, that far away?
Creative and clever, this I must say!

His name is Dave, the man you'll wed.
Get back to you soon, my cell phone is dead!

Janet are you there, where were we now?
Of course we can come, your wedding, oh WOW!

So Dave is our man, your text is quite clear,
Attractive and tall, the man of the year!

He's smitten with you, smart lad indeed.
You're a catch, my lady, you do take the lead!

A toast to this couple, support them we do.
Their future is bright, their love so true!

Cameron House-Loch Lomond, Scotland

RW Van Dyke - My Mentor

RW Van Dyke, a legend he is,
When driving a bus, the macadam is his.

For sixty five years behind the wheel,
All the girl's hearts, RW did steal.

The United States, the roads he does know,
Some wild oats, this driver did sow.

"RW, I'm lost, Miami is here,
Collins Avenue the beach, help me I fear."

"Coliseum I'm seeking, just how do I go?"
"Take the road son, take the road you know!"

A wise-crack from him, humor at the front,
Bus driver, me too, for the road I will hunt!

World War II, Robert Warren Van Dyke,
Many medals were awarded to this man we like!

Presidential Citation, FDR back then,
A medal for combat, this war we did win!

RW the hero, a Bronze Star to him,
Americans they were, must our thoughts not dim!

Tenth Armored Division, in France he was,
Feeding ammo, machine gun, thirty caliber he does.

He rode in a half track, twelve soldiers in all,
These men fought hard, they walked so tall!

Get back to this man, my friend indeed,
Honky Tonks in his teens, he did take the lead.

Living with Grandparents, a wonderful pair,
Sometimes on his own, but these people did care!

Confidence he had, many places he's been,
Personality was his, pour a glass of gin!

Rarely you will see so determined a man,
Continental Trailways, back then it began.

Mile after mile and day after day,
Orange cones, yellow stripes, the tolls he did pay.

Kansas City to Denver, thirty six was the road,
Dropping papers in Bird City, it was part of his load.

Throw a remark at RW, and watch him respond,
His wit is quick, a friend you will bond!

Injectors, pistons and Jake brakes he knows,
Mechanics or driving, where trouble he goes!

Twenty four seven, this man is on call,
A sweetheart in bed, the cell phone his doll.

The ring comes in, "We have a bus that's down!"
Fifty people on board, "Your location, what town?"

"It's freezing out here, our engine has blown!"
"Patrolman has arrived, our emergency is known!"

At two in the morning, RW springs to life,
Rabbit Ears Pass, cut the tension with a knife!

"A motorcoach we'll need, Steamboat is near,
Time is the essence, it's frostbite we fear!"

Cell phone to his ear, the number he knows,
The rescue is made, driver's face just glows!!

One in a million, RW stands out,
A salute to this man whom we say has clout!

From London to St. Louis,
Chuck's final professional flight.

Chuck Shull Airline Pilot M-14

Eight hundred times, the Atlantic he crossed,
This boy is a pilot, no time he has lost.

From a fifty five Chevy to a seven six seven,
This kid flew the planes just this side of heaven!

The lad was wild, he rubbed off on me,
At times I know from the cops he'd flee!

His fifty five Chevy, a legend oh my,
Sped through the counties, this car did fly.

Cubic inches by Chevy, three hundred forty eight,
A car built for racing, just open the gate!

Chuck was tough, and football he played,
He was an ace, he was a spade.

Hap Shull his Dad, a bomber he flew,
Aviation in their blood, a dedicated few!

To Bird City Chuck came, in the seventh grade,
Best friends we were, our plans were made.

Stories we have that cannot be told,
So many a blur, let some unfold.

A small town indeed, maybe boring it was,
Attracted to the standpipe, I say just because.

We climbed this tower many times in all,
On the edge we lived, we could take a fall.

(continued)

Shall I tell this Chuck, it's you I expose?
The bullets, they sounded like stereo by Bose!

Forget this tale, move on with life,
We all have fun, we all have strife.

Chuck Shull a pilot, twenty one years old,
For TWA, third youngest I'm told.

From a small town in Kansas to the world he came,
Everywhere he flew, this was his game.

All around our planet and over the top,
Bangkok and Hong Kong, these places he'd stop.

New York to Paris, again and again,
Experience he built, his wings he did win!

TWA, thirty six years, American for two,
Also hobbies he did have, model airplanes too.

Many years this career, some excitement was had,
An engine on fire, when he was only a lad!

Another close call, collecting ice on his wings,
Down close to warm water, this plane he brings.

Who knows how many lives a pilot does save?
The adrenaline, quick thinking, their decisions are brave!

Chuck Shull a captain, this remarkable career,
From Cessna to Boeing, forty years we do cheer!

Answer from page 54...propeller.

Made in the USA
Columbia, SC
28 September 2017